Tax law and public finance in Rwanda

Collection « Droits, Sociétés, Politiques - Afrique des Grands Lacs »

Collection dirigée par Jean-François Boudet

Limitée à un espace géographique donné, la Collection « Droits, Sociétés, Politiques - Afrique des Grands Lacs » accueille des ouvrages scientifiques et professionnels de qualité, écrits autant par des juristes que des économistes, des historiens, des politistes, des philosophes ou des sociologues, contribuant à la publication et à la diffusion d'ouvrages ainsi que des outils pédagogiques au service du Droit et de la construction de la Paix dans la région des Grands Lacs.

Déjà parus

Éric DAVID, *Génocide au Rwanda, Les enquêtes officielles menées en Belgique, en France, à l'ONU et à l'OUA*, 2015.

Pie HABIMANA

TAX LAW AND PUBLIC FINANCE IN RWANDA

Preface Jean-François BOUDET

Postface Jean Baptiste TWAHIRWA

L'HARMATTAN

5-7, rue de l'École-Polytechnique ; 75005 Paris
http://www.harmattan.fr
diffusion.harmattan@wanadoo.fr
harmattan1@wanadoo.fr
ISBN : 978-2-343-06843-5
EAN : 9782343068435

Dedicated to my wife Antoinette and my son Igor Darron

List of abbreviations

AG	: Auditor General
CBM	: Chief Budget Manager
COMESA	: Common Market for Eastern and Southern Africa
EAC	: East African Community
FTZ	: Free Trade Zone
INTOSAI	: International Organization of the Supreme Audit Institutions
IPAR	: Institute of Policy Analysis and Research
MINECOFIN	: Ministry of Economic Finance
OAG	: Office of Auditor General
OBL	: Organic Budget Law
OECD	: Organisation for Economic Cooperation and Development
O.G.	: Official Gazette
RRA	: Rwanda Revenue Authority
SAI	: Supreme Audit Institutions
SADC	: Southern African Development Community
SEZ	: Special Economic Zone
SEZAR	: Special Economic Zone Regulatory Authority
TIN	: Taxpayer Identification Number
TSA	: Treasury Single Account
UNCTAD	: United Nations Conference on Trade and Development
USD	: American dollars
VAT	: Value Added Tax

Table of Contents

List of abbreviations 9
Preface 15
Introduction 19
CHAPTER ONE: THE MANAGEMENT OF PUBLIC FINANCES IN RWANDA 21
I.1. Rwanda Legal framework of public finances 23
I.1.1. Constitution 23
I.1.2. Organic budget law 25
I.1.3. Annual budget laws 26
I.2. Institutional framework of public finances 27
I.2.1. The Ministry of finance 28
I.2.2. The Parliament 29
I.2.3. Office of Auditor General of State Finances 29
I.3. Budget planning, execution and control in Rwanda .. 31
I.3.1. Compliance with budgetary principles 31
I.3.2. Budget planning and preparation 32
I.3.3. Budget execution 32
I.3.4. Government oversight arrangements 33
I.4. Government banking arrangements 34
CHAPTER TWO: THE RWANDAN TAX LAW 37
II.1. Historical background of taxation in Rwanda 39
II.2. Main principles governing tax in Rwanda 43
II.2.1. Constitutional principles 43
II.2.1.1. The principle of legality of tax 43
II.2.1.2. The principle of equality before tax 44
II.2.1.3. The principle of liberty 45
II.2.2. Non-constitutional principles 45
II.2.2.1. The principle of non-retroactivity 45
II.2.2.2. The principle of territoriality 46
II.3. Rwandan tax structure 47
II.3.1. Centralized taxes 47
II.3.1.1. Value Added Tax (VAT) 48
II.3.1.1.1. Historical background 48
II.3.1.1.2. VAT Registration 48
II.3.1.1.3. VAT taxable activities 49

II.3.1.1.4. VAT standard rate and time for payment 49
II.3.1.1.5. Zero rate VAT and exonerations 50
II.3.1.2. Direct taxes on income 51
II.3.1.2.1. Personal income tax 51
II.3.1.2.1.1. Business profits 51
II.3.1.2.1.2. Investment income 56
II.3.1.2.2. Corporate Income Tax 58
II.3.1.2.3. Withholding taxes 60
II.3.1.2.3.1. Pay as You Earn (PAYE) tax 60
II.3.1.2.3.2. Withholding Tax on Imports and public Tenders 63
II.3.1.2.3.3. Withholding Tax on other payments 64
II.3.1.2.4. Property tax: 4th base: boats 64
II.3.1.2.5. Registration fees for vehicles 65
II.3.1.2.6. Consumption taxes (Excise Taxes) 65
II.3.1.2.7. Import Duties 66
II.3.2. Decentralized taxes 67
II.3.2.1. Property tax 67
II.3.2.1.1. 1st base: Registered occupied houses 67
II.3.2.1.2. 2nd base: Area of unbuilt plots 69
II.3.2.1.3. 6th base: Mineral concessions 70
II.3.2.2. Tax on rental revenues 71
II.3.2.3. Trading Licence Tax 72
II.4. Tax incentives under Rwandan law 75
II.4.1. Profit tax discount 75
II.4.2. Investment allowance 76
II.4.3. Research and development tax incentives 77
II.4.4. Tax holidays 77
II.4.5. Tax incentives in Special Economic Zones 78
II.5. Tax procedure and tax litigation in Rwanda 80
II.5.1. The taxpayers' duties 80
II.5.1.1. Filing tax returns 80
II.5.1.1.1. Rectification 80
II.5.1.1.2. Audit and investigations 81
II.5.1.1.3. Entrance to premises without notice 83
II.5.1.1.4. Estimated assessment procedure 83

II.5.1.1.5. Extending the deadline for filing tax returns 84
II.5.1.2. Paying the due tax 85
II.5.1.2.1. Possibility of paying taxes in instalments ... 85
II.5.1.2.2. Waive of tax liability, interest and penalties 86
II.5.1.2.3. Prescription 87
II.5.1.3. Other duties of taxpayer 87
II.5.1.3.1. Duty to register 87
II.5.1.3.2. Duty to register for VAT 87
II.5.1.3.3. Duty to use prescribed VAT invoice 88
II.5.2. Fiscal litigation: Settlement of fiscal disputes ... 88
II.5.2.1. The procedure for centralised taxes 88
II.5.2.1.1. Administrative appeal 88
II.5.2.1.2. Judicial appeal 89
II.5.2.2. The procedure for decentralised taxes 89
II.5.2.2.1. Administrative appeal 90
II.5.2.2.2. Judicial appeal 90
II.5.3. Evidences in tax law 90
II.5.3.1. The burden of proof 90
II.5.3.2. Types of evidences 92
II.5.3.2.1. Ordinary evidences 92
II.5.3.2.2. Signs and indications of prosperity 92
II.5.3.2.3. Affidavits 93
II.5.4. Fiscal sanctions 94
II.5.4.1. Sanctions applicable to centralised taxes 94
II.5.4.1.1. Sanctions imposed by tax administration 94
II.5.4.1.2. Sanctions imposed by the courts 99
II.5.4.2. Sanctions applicable to decentralised taxes 99
II.5.5. Forced recovery 100
II.5.5.1. The procedure for centralised taxes 100
II.5.5.1.1. Warning 100
II.5.5.1.2. Seizure and auction of taxpayer's property 101
II.5.5.1.3. Notification to third parties 101
II.5.5.2. The procedure for descentralised taxes 102
II.5.5.2.1. Warning 102

II.5.5.2.2. Seizure and auction of taxpayer's property 102
II.5.5.2.3. Notification to third parties 103
II.6. International aspects of Rwanda tax system 103
II.6.1. Permanent establishment under Rwandan law 103
II.6.2. Taxation of electronic commerce in Rwanda .. 104
II.6.3. EAC regional integration and impact on taxes 105
Postface 111
References 131

Preface

On dit habituellement qu'il y a eu autant de publications sur le Rwanda entre le moment de l'indépendance et 1994 qu'entre celui du génocide perpétré contre les Tutsis et 2014. Encore un ouvrage sur le pays des mille collines, me direz-vous che(è)r(e) lecteur(rice) ! C'est vrai. Et, pourtant la monographie de Me Pie HABIMANA, jeune enseignant-chercheur à l'Université du Rwanda, est originale tant sur la forme que sur le fond : elle s'intitule *Tax law and Public finance in Rwanda*. L'ouvrage respecte tout d'abord l'orientation constitutionnelle prise en juin 2003 consistant en l'introduction à part égale des langues officielles que sont le kinyarwanda, le français et l'anglais. La préface est ainsi rédigée en français, le corps du texte en anglais et la postface en kinyarwanda.

Le travail de Me Pie HABIMANA est ensuite une œuvre complète de description de droit des finances publiques rwandais ; et c'est peut-être là son apport essentiel : il présente l'organisation budgétaire au Rwanda (chapitre 1) pour mieux comprendre le droit fiscal du pays (chapitre 2). Cette étude constitue ainsi une véritable rupture positiviste et constructive du droit des finances publiques rwandais. Il manquerait certes des développements plus conséquents sur les rapports financiers qu'entretient le Rwanda avec les communautés régionales et les Etats limitrophes, des débats sur le rôle de l'impôt en tant que pourvoyeur de fonds publics ou des questionnements sur la fiscalité coloniale et post-génocidaire, mais l'auteur entend davantage introduire ici le droit des finances publiques rwandaises pour l'avenir. Il n'y a rien d'étonnant à affirmer cela car Me Pie HABIMANA fait partie de cette nouvelle génération de juristes rwandais formés après 1994 et imprégnés de la culture financière belge et française à la une du système anglo-saxon et de la globalisation financière.

Cette étude constitue alors, che(è)r(e) lecteur(rice), une double promesse : celle de la confiance et celle de la fidélité. Deux valeurs essentielles pour la reconstruction générale d'un pays meurtri mais debout et de tout système politique et financier en particulier. Car, c'est bien ce que nous apprend la lecture de l'ouvrage de Me Pie HABIMANA : la structure des finances publiques au Rwanda est toujours perfectible mais elle s'assoit manifestement sur une volonté de créer une dynamique budgétaire et fiscale afin d'accroître l'indépendance du pays à l'égard des bailleurs de fonds publics et privés et d'attirer les investisseurs étrangers dans l'appareil productif rwandais. Cette première monographie mérite sans nul doute une suite à donner – mais ce n'est qu'un encouragement et une invitation – pour mieux comprendre ce présent tourné vers l'avenir en s'appuyant sur le passé. Œuvres de résilience et d'humilité pour toute une vie.

Nul besoin de rappeler ces qualités au peuple rwandais et à l'auteur du présent ouvrage. Que Me Pie HABIMANA soit donc remercié d'être entré dans la belle aventure académique par la grande porte de la publication de sa recherche et qu'il poursuive toujours cet effort pour transmettre sa passion du droit des finances publiques aux générations futures, notamment à Kigali et à Butare, participant ainsi à sa manière aux dialogues des cultures.

Jean-François BOUDET
Maître de conférences (HDR) en Droit public
Université Sorbonne Paris Cité
CMH (Paris Descartes)
Associé au CERSA (CNRS – Université Paris II UMR7106)
Collaborateur scientifique au CMAP (Université catholique de Louvain)
et au Tax Institute (Université de Liège)

Introduction

Public finance simply refers to the resources and expenditures of the State. The law of public finance refers to that branch of public law regulating the ways and means of collection of funds for the government as well as the way and means the collected funds are used by the government.

Area of public finance in Rwanda covers the resources and expenditures of the State *per se* i.e. the central government as well as the local entities and public institutions also referred to as semi-public institutions or public entities or public establishments. Under Rwandan law, a public institution is defined as an institution enjoying a legal personality and managed in accordance with laws governing public service, to which the State allocates funds in order for it to carry out specialised activities for public interest.[1] The responsibilities, category, organisation, management and functioning of such institutions are governed by the laws establishing them.[2]

Having a legal personality, public institution enjoy administrative and financial autonomy and report to a public supervising authority, in most cases a ministry having related attributions. The supervising authority, the category as well as the structure of a public institution are determined by the law establishing the concerned institution. In most cases, the law[3] refers to a ministerial order or a prime minister order to determine the structure, the category and the supervising authority.

---

[1] Art. 2 of the Organic Law n° 34/2007 of 13/08/2007 modifying and complementing the Organic Law n° 14/2004 of 26/05/2004 establishing general provisions governing public institutions, in *O.G.* n° 16 of 15/08/2004.

[2] *Ibid.*

[3] A public institution can be created by a law or an organic law.

The public finances are submitted to a rigorous legal regime different from the private finances. Summarily, the two finances are different from two crucial aspects namely the governing principles and the pursued objectives. In fact, the rules and principles governing the two are quite different due to the fact that the financing system of the privates is limited and narrowed, while the financing system of the State and its organs is generally too wide. And, even if some multinational corporations can have a large amount of business, this cannot reach the business managed by the State and its organs. The two finances also pursue different objectives. Private persons are only concerned with the satisfaction of their interest whereas the State's concern is the satisfaction of the general or public interest. In this regard, it doesn't matter whether the profit is little or zero, what matters is the satisfaction of the general interest.

From the above differences, the management of public finances requires an existence and application of some special rules that are not applicable to the management of private finances. The intervention of the law in public finance refers to a set of constitutional and administrative rules that regulate the collection of funds for the State and the expenditure of collected funds by the State. The Rwandan legislator intervene to regulate public finances by issuing legal framework governing the budget, taxes and State debts, the procedures of receipts and expenditures of the State, etc.

The first chapter of this part deals with the regulation of public finances in Rwanda before concentrating to the second chapter that concentrates on the regulation of taxes in Rwanda, as a major source of public finances.

CHAPTER ONE

THE MANAGEMENT OF PUBLIC FINANCES IN RWANDA

Introduction

Rwanda's public financial management system is established through a set regulatory framework and institutional framework. The legal framework of public finances in Rwanda is led by the Constitution at the apex of a three-tier legislative framework. The Constitution also provides for the Organic Budget Law and Ordinary Laws, commonly referred to as annual finance law. The institutional framework of public finances in Rwanda is characterised by a number of institutions intervening in public finance on complementarity basis.

I.1. Rwanda Legal framework of public finances

The regulation of public finances in Rwanda is organised through different legal instruments governing this domain, from the Constitution as the supreme law of the land to instructions from different competent organs.

I.1.1. Constitution

The current Constitution of the Republic of Rwanda was adopted on 04th June 2003 by a way of referendum. So far, it has been amended four times. The 2003 Constitution defines the principles and overall legal framework for the management of public finances in Rwanda. Article 79 of the Constitution sets out the roles and responsibilities in respect of submission of the draft Finance Law by Cabinet, the adoption of the Finance Law by Parliament, and the submission of a budget execution report to the Auditor General of the State Finance. Article 91 of the same Constitution limits the legislature's ability to modify the Finance Act by providing that "Bills and statutory amendments which have the potential to reduce Government revenue or increase State expenditure must indicate proposals for raising the required revenue or making savings equivalent to the anticipated expenditure". Such a provision contributes to fiscal discipline as it sets limits for the Parliament to adopt a law which may have an impact on State finances without having a projection on the compensation.

Article 128 of the Constitution grants the power to the Parliament to obtain information and exercise oversight of activities of the government, and provides for an organic law to determine the procedures for this oversight. It is through this government activities oversight that the Parliament enjoys the power to oversee any government activity relating to public finance.

As usual, the 2003 Rwandan Constitution does not provide details on budget preparation. With respect to timing, the Constitution does not expressly specify that the Chamber of Deputies must adopt the budget before the beginning of the fiscal year. However, for the sake of preventing a government shutdown in case the budget is not adopted in a timely manner, the Constitution expressly provides that "in the event that the finance bill is not voted and promulgated before the commencement of a financial year, the Prime Minister authorizes by an order a monthly expenditure on a provisional basis of an amount equal to one twelfth of the budget of the preceding year".[4]

Regarding the budget execution for the previous year, the Constitution requires the Cabinet to submit, before 30th June of the following year, to the Chamber of Deputies a finance bill with a report on implementation of the budget, certified by the Auditor General of State finance. To achieve this deadline, the Cabinet has an obligation to submit a report on the implementation of the budget to the Auditor General not later than 31st March of the following financial year. This means that under Rwandan law, the

[4] Art. 80 of the Constitution of 04th June 2003 as amended to date, in *O.G.* n° special of 04th June 2003.

constitutionally-mandated reporting of the budget is ex-post reporting, meaning that an obligation to report concerns only the previous year and not the current year.

Important to note is that the Constitution of the Republic of Rwanda does not impose any quantitative "fiscal rules", such as limiting public sector debt to a specific amount or requiring a zero-deficit budget over economic cycle. What it does in this matter is only to limit the parliament to adopt laws having an impact on State finances by setting an obligation to have a projection on compensation.

I.1.2. Organic budget law

In 2006, the Rwandan legislator has adopted the organic law n° 37/2006 of 12/09/2006 on State finances and property[5] commonly referred to as Organic Budget Law (OBL). This organic budget law provides a strong framework for public finance management in Rwanda by defining the roles and responsibilities of institutions and individuals as well as providing them with guidance relating to procedures to be followed. This law prescribes in more specific terms the controls and administrative framework for the management and accounting for public funds. It vests the authority and responsibility for supervision of the collection and use of public funds in the Minister responsible for Finance and economic planning.

For purposes of operating the central government budget, the OBL establishes a consolidated fund, which constitutes all revenues and other public monies, including earmarked revenues of extra-budgetary funds, and external loans and grants raised or received for the purpose of, or on behalf, of the central government. Consequently, the Minister and public officers, following Parliamentary

---

[5] *O.G.* n° special of 12/09/2006.

approval: (i) may only use the appropriated funds for authorized purposes; (ii) may not incur expenditure in excess of the appropriated funds; and (iii) must use the appropriated funds within the financial year. The OBL also sets out general guiding principles relating to the preparation and implementation of budgets.

The OBL is made of seven parts corresponding to seven titles, each focusing on a specific matter. In addition to part one that sets out the general principles governing public finance management, part two of this law sets out the powers of the various actors in Public Finance management while part three provides for the preparation, presentation and approval of budgets. Part four of this organic law addresses budget execution and part five regulates the government borrowing, debt management and banking arrangements. Part six of the OBL concerns accounting, reporting and auditing provisions and finally comes Part seven which is about situations requiring special provisions like offences, penalties, amendments, etc.

For accountability and control purposes, the Minister of finance and economic planning is, every year, required to seek the authority of Parliament to use funds for specified purposes by submitting an annual Finance Law.

I.1.3. Annual budget laws

For accountability and control purposes, the Minister is required to seek the authority of Parliament to use funds for specified purposes by submitting an annual Finance Law. It is in this perspective that every year the parliament passes a law on budget. This is provided for by article 79 of the Constitution according to which "every financial year, the chamber of deputies adopts the State finance law". The same article further reads that before the commencement of the session devoted to the examination of the Budget, the Cabinet submits to both chambers of the Parliament the finance bill for the coming financial year, and the Parliament receives the Budget implementation report for the first semester of the current financial year presented to it by the Cabinet before examining the budget of the next financial year. In the same regard, before the commencement of the session devoted to the examination of the Budget, the Auditor General of State Finances also submits to the Parliament the audited state consolidated financial statements of the previous financial year.[6]

Even if the finance bill is submitted to both chambers, the examination of relevance is carried out by the Chamber of Deputies only. However, before the final adoption of the Budget, the Senate must provide the Chamber of Deputies with its opinion on the State Finance Bill.[7] In the event the finance bill is not voted and promulgated before the commencement of a financial year, the Prime Minister authorises by an order a monthly expenditure on a provisional basis of an amount equal to one-twelfth of the budget of the preceding year.[8]

I.2. Institutional framework of public finances

Area of public finance in Rwanda is managed by a large network of different institutions that intervene in one way or another. Most of them are public institutions or semi-public institutions. A few number of private institutions intervene in public finance management but their role is limited and not direct.

---

[6] Art. 79 paragraph 5 of the Constitution.
[7] Art. 79 paragraph 6 of the Constitution.
[8] Art. 80 of the Constitution.

I.2.1. The Ministry of finance

The Ministry of finance plays a major role in public finance in Rwanda. First and foremost, it is the ministry of finance that prepares the annual finance bill.[9] The minister of finance also serves the role of chief manager of the revenues and the expenditures in the central Government consolidated fund after consultation with the Public Treasury Management Committee.[10] With this role, article 9 of the OBL expressly specify that any withdrawal of funds from the consolidated fund in the central Government must not be done, except under written permission issued by the Minister of finance.

The minister of finance also has a number of responsibilities relating to public finances such as advising the Government on budgetary policies; promoting good preparation of the budget, its management, execution, public accounting and fiscal reporting on the use on the State finances; ensuring within the resources available, efficient cash management to equitably meet the budgetary spending requirements; coordinate, supervise and monitor the management of Government assets and liabilities; promoting and enforcing transparency and accountability in budget management; ensuring that Parliament is kept informed on macroeconomic and budgetary developments; etc.[11]

According to article 19 of the OBL, the Minister of finance is the paymaster for overall expenditures in all State services as the President of the Republic is the overall paymaster of the State Budget. The Minister of finance can also propose the Government to borrow loans as he/she has authority to choose the form of loan and to

---

[9] Art. 11.4° of the OBL.
[10] Art. 7 paragraph 3 of the OBL.
[11] Art. 12 of the OBL.

approve the terms of bowing in consultation with the Central Bank.[12]

I.2.2. The Parliament

The Constitution of the Republic of Rwanda requires the Cabinet to submit to Parliament the finance bill for the concerned financial year with a report on the implementation of the budget for the previous year certified by the Auditor General. Annual accounts are to be presented to the Auditor General and to Parliament within three months after the end of the financial year, and the audit report should be completed, and submitted to Parliament, within six months after the end of the financial year. The Auditor-General is required to prepare a report including his/her audit opinion and to submit it to each Chamber of Parliament. Parliament may also instruct the Office of the Auditor General to carry out a financial audit of any institution of the State or with regard to the use of funds provided for by the State.

I.2.3. Office of Auditor General of State Finances

The Office of Auditor General of State Finances (OAG) also greatly intervenes in public finance management in Rwanda. This Office was created by the law n° 04/98 of 04th June 1998. This law conferred upon the OAG the authority to conduct, in its capacity as the country's supreme audit institution, an audit of all state finances and to report to Parliament on the stewardship of Government and the management of public funds.

This authority of the OAG is also enshrined in the Constitution that confers upon it the responsibility for the audit of state finances, and vests it with a legal personality and financial and administrative autonomy. The

---

[12] Art. 57 of the OBL.

Constitution specifies that the OAG is an independent national institution responsible for the audit of State finances.[13] The independence of the OAG is guaranteed by prohibiting any State interference in the functioning of the Office. As well, the responsibilities of the Office are also stated in the constitution.[14]

Each year, the Auditor-General is required to submit to each Chamber of Parliament, prior to the commencement of the session devoted to the examination of the budget of the following year a complete report on the implementation of the State budget of the previous year. This report must indicate the manner in which the budget was utilized, expenses which were contrary to the law and whether there was misappropriation of public funds. A copy of the report must be submitted to the President of the Republic, the Cabinet, the President of the Supreme Court and the Prosecutor General.

In Rwanda, the OAG is headed by the Auditor General (AG) assisted by a Deputy Auditor General. The Auditor General is appointed for a renewable period of five years by the President of the Republic, after Cabinet consultations. The appointment, together with that of the deputy, is subject to the approval of the Senate. The OAG is organized into six departments and services, each headed by a Director and such departments are the Department of Central Government, the Department of Local Government, the Department of Projects and Programs, the Department of the Autonomous Public Companies, the Department of Synthesis and Programs[15]

---

[13] Art. 183 of the Constitution.

[14] *Ibidem.*

[15] This department is responsible for the syntheses of audit reports, drafting of the reports, legal affairs, research, co-operation and continuous training.

and the Department of Administration and Finance. The OAG is a member of the International Organization of the Supreme Audit Institutions (INTOSAI)[16] and adheres to its principles in the conduct of its work.

I.3. Budget planning, execution and control in Rwanda

The budget process in Rwanda follows a number of principles and different measures have been set to control its effective implementation.

I.3.1. Compliance with budgetary principles

There exist a number of principles that govern the budgeting system. The main of those principles, applicable in Rwanda, are the principle of annuality, the principle of budgetary unit, the principle of budgetary universality, the principle of loans specificity, etc. As far the annuality is concerned, the budget in Rwanda is considered on yearly basis, i.e. on a period of 12 months. In Rwanda, like in other EAC member countries, the budget year starts on 01st July and ends on 30th June.[17] The budget in Rwanda is established in one document containing all receipts and expenditures (budgetary unit) and the entire amount of resources must cover the entire amount of expenditures (budget universality). Contrary to other sources of income for the Government, loans are contracted to cover a specific service or a determined service (loans specificity).

---

[16] INTOSAI is an international organization that groups supreme audit institutions (SAI) in countries that belong to the United Nations. It plays a major role is setting international auditing standards and helping member Supreme Audit Institutions (SAIs) to adhere to them. INTOSAI supports its members in this task by providing training to staff and opportunities to share information and experiences about modern auditing and evaluation techniques.

[17] Rwanda, before joining EAC the budget year used to start on 01st January and end on 31st December and Rwanda changed as matter of harmonizing its budget with other EAC members States.

I.3.2. Budget planning and preparation

The budget planning and preparation is mainly the duty of the ministry of finance and economic planning. This ministry coordinates budget planning and preparation efforts from different government organs and institutions. In fact, each government organ and institution sets out its budget and these budgets go up to the next head line management up to the ministry levels and end in the ministry of finance and economic planning, which establishes the final draft budget to be submitted to the parliament for approval and adoption of the law to that purpose.

The budget planning refers to a strategic plan, setting out expenditure and deficit targets, on the basis of macroeconomic projections, ideally over 3 to 5 years. Within this framework, medium-term policy targets and expenditure priorities are specified. This is the process of national planning and forms the building blocks of a medium-term expenditure framework (MTEF).

The budget preparation consists in submission and negotiation of ministry expenditure bids within budget guidelines and expenditure limits circulated by the ministry of finance and economic planning. This stage culminates in preparation of the budget by the ministry of finance that is submitted to the parliament for review and legislative approval.

I.3.3. Budget execution

When the budget appropriations are approved, resources are released to the spending agencies to implement expenditure programs. In Rwanda, the budget execution mainly falls in the hands of the Chief Budget Managers. The term Chief Budget Manager (CBM) refers to the administrative head of the budget in the budget agency or any other civil servant such a manager delegates.[18] The Chief Budget Managers of governmental budget agencies are provided for in article 20 of the OBL.[19]

CBMs are responsible for implementing the government's agreed policies, including the preparation and execution of the budgets for their agencies and for the accountability on the use of public resources. It is the duty of the CBMs to make judgments related to the appropriateness of the expenditure and of the authority to initiate the expense. For instance, CBMs also verify that suppliers have fulfilled their contractual obligations. They issue purchase orders, verify the delivery of goods and services, verify the amount payable in respect of these and prepare and submit payment requests.

I.3.4. Government oversight arrangements

The oversight of the public finance environment is basically exercised by three institutions namely the Parliament, the internal audit function within Government, and the Office of the Auditor General of State Finance. The 2003 Constitution confers upon Parliament the duty to examine and approve the annual finance law, and requires

---

[18] Art. 2.8⁰ of the OBL.

[19] According to art. 20 of the OBL, the chief budget manager for a budget agency are the Director of cabinet in the office of the President of the Republic, the secretary general of Senate in the Parliament, the Clerk of the Chamber of Deputies in the Parliament, the director of Cabinet in the Prime Minister's Office, the Secretary General in the Supreme Court, the Secretary General in National Prosecution Services, the Secretary General in each Ministry, the first Counselor in the Embassy or any other authorized officer in the Embassy approved by the Minister, the Director in charge of finance in the Office of the Ombudsman, the Executive Secretary of the Province, the Executive Secretary of Kigali City, the Executive Secretary of National Commission, the Director of a Public enterprise using State Budget, the Executive Secretary in Local administrative entities, any other lawfully authorized officer.

the annual budget execution reports and financial statements to be submitted to it.

Before 1998, the external audit of state finances was entrusted to the Court of Accounts. Starting with 1998, the Government introduced the Office of the Auditor General of State Finance to take responsibility for external audit of Government accounts. This position was later reinforced through the promulgation of the new Constitution in 2003 which effectively abolished the Court of Accounts.

In addition, although internal auditors were established in line ministries and public institutions, their roles are limited to internal control activities, ensuring that internal control procedures are observed and respected. Their duties are overwhelmingly of a pre-audit nature, compromising their independence from the normal day-to-day operational decisions of the budget agencies to which they are assigned.

The Constitution confers upon parliament the role of reviewing Government's budget management decisions. It has the right to propose amendments on the composition of the proposed budget, but not to change the overall fiscal deficit. Its propositions will not be admissible if their adoption results in the reduction of revenues or an increase in public expenditures, unless they are accompanied by a proposal to increase revenues or make equivalent savings of expenditures. Parliament also has the right to review the budget execution report and the financial statements.

I.4. Government banking arrangements

There has been a gradual proliferation of bank accounts during past years. The 2002 Report on the Public Sector

Bank Accounts[20] listed 1,468 bank accounts opened in the name of various government institutions. With the exception of line ministries, whose salaries and larger payments for goods and services and investments financed from internal resources are paid directly out of the main treasury account, most institutions receive funds from the budget into their bank account(s) and make their own payments. The existence of such a disproportionately large number of accounts for a small administration impedes the efficient management of treasury resources by Government. As a result, the Treasury's ability to routinely monitor balances on accounts outside its control and effectively to manage the government's overall cash position has been impaired. This lack of control also led to significant difficulties in reconciling its fiscal and monetary accounts.

The Government has sought to put in place measures to reduce this proliferation and thus to strengthen management in this area. It has issued instructions to close all bank accounts that are considered to be dormant. The OBL contains specific provisions for the Minister of Finance to approve establishment of all government bank accounts. These measures aim to strengthen Treasury oversight and include the move towards the establishment of a Treasury Single Account (TSA).

The introduction of the Treasury Single Account in the OBL and government's efforts to effect these provisions represent a significant step in the normalization of the treasury management system. It is envisaged that the TSA enables centralized payments to be made, thus enhancing the cash management system. It also enables the provision

---

[20] *Rapport de l'Etude sur les Comptes Bancaires du Secteur Public*, GN & Partners, for MINECOFIN, October 2002.

of information that facilitates the reconciliation of fiscal and monetary records.

According to OBL, in its article 16, all raised or received central Government money must be credited into a single treasury account in the National Bank of Rwanda and the Minister in charge of finance must ensure that there is sufficient money in the TSA at all times before payments are authorized. The TSA may include sub-accounts for specific Government transactions and where necessary, treasury transit accounts may be opened in any other bank, including commercial banks, upon approval by the ministry in charge of finance.

With a view to facilitate the Government receipts, the minister in charge of finance, on behalf of the State, may enter into an agreement with any bank, including commercial banks, on matters relating to receipts, custody, payment or transfers of public money, or any other matter relating to Government transactions with the bank.[21] It is in this regard that for instance, presently, centralized taxes are paid through the Bank of Kigali Ltd if not paid directly to Rwanda Revenue Authority agents.[22]

It is important to note that Extra-budgetary funds operated by central government like the Road Fund, National AIDS Commission, etc do not fall within the scope of the TSA. These funds have their own bank accounts and usually have sources of finance additional to the budgetary transfers, often donor funds. They make their own payments and their accounts are generally not integrated into the government's accounts.

---

[21] Art. 16 *in fine* of the law on Budget 2013-2014.

[22] Other examples include the payments to University of Rwanda, a public institution, which are done via the I&M Bank Ltd or ECOBANK Ltd.

CHAPTER TWO

THE RWANDAN TAX LAW

Introduction

Like in other countries, taxes constitute one of the factors contributing to the viability of Rwanda. Taxes in Rwanda, even though not contributing a major part of State resources, it matters a lot studying this important element that any government counts on to survive.

II.1. Historical background of taxation in Rwanda

Taxes in Rwanda have got almost the same history like in other societies. Especially the notions of religion and war were the major justifications of taxes in ancient Rwanda. In fact, in ancient Rwanda, the King (le *Mwami*) was not only a political administrator but also a religious chief governing according to the will of the god. Therefore, for Rwandans, contributing to his governance was not contrary to the divine will.

In addition to complying with divine will, in ancient Rwanda, people used to pay what was called *ikoro ry'umuheto* and these were contributions oriented to the financing of wars. This was mainly influenced by the wars that were frequent and which wars were conducted in the name and for account of Rwandan citizens. Obviously, these citizens were obligated to contribute to the success of those wars. The contributions were either in nature (physical services) or through payment of harvest like sorghums, beans or domestic animals.

However, a person can challenge the consideration of such contributions as taxes, basically saying that they were of little value to finance public expenditures. To theses critics, we refer to C. Kalinijabo according to who, taxes are appreciated, qualified and justified reference made to the function of their final objective, being economic, financial or social[23] and not to its quantity or volume. Again, one cannot categorically say that these contributions were of little value considering the value of contributions to the economic level of the time. For instance, the following table shows the contributions given to the King Musinga in 1926.

Contributions given to King Musinga in 1926

Item	**Quantity**	**Price/unit**	**Total value in Rwf**
Old hoes (*amafuni*)	428	1,00	428
New hoes (*imijyojyo*)	2,758	6	16,548
Beans and peas	1,373	15kg to 6 Rwf	8,238
Sorghum	684	5kg to 1,5 Rwf	1,026
Eleusine	90	0,3 per kg	27
Jug of honey (*imitsama*)	1,059	6 per small jug	6,354
Jug of honey beer (ubuki)	411	3 per small jug	1,233
Jug of banana beer (*urwagwa*)	509	3 per ordinary jug	1,527
Ibisabo	60	5	300
Ibyansi	81	1	81
Ibicuba	8	4	32
Inkangara	40	1	40
Intango	2	2	4
Wood Plates *(imbehe)*	40	0,50	20

---

[23] C. Kalinijabo, *op. cit.*, n° 254, cited in Nikozitambirwa, "De l'Impot Ikoro", available at http://users.skynet.be/wihogora/niko-rmm-ikoro-020503.htm, accessed on 15th June 2011.

Amamana y'inka	122	80	9,760
Amamana y'intama	68	6	408
Machete (*imihoro*)	69	5	345
Axes (*intorezo*)	4	6	24
Imitana	153	5	765
Allows (*imishale*)	231	3 for 1 Rwf	77
Arches (*imiheto*)	20	1	20
Spears (*amacumu*)	142	3	426
Small knives (*ingongo*)	17	1	17
Impuzu	4	1	4
Carpets (*ibirago*)	3,559	2	7,118
Perfums (*imibavu*)	17	10	170
Antilope skins	357	5	1,735
Bracelet (*ubutega*)	189	25	4,725
Iron bracelet (*inyereri*)	36	35	1,260
Shells (*ibitungu*)	29	5	145
Pearls (*inigi*)	1.1	1	1.1
TOTAL			**63,957 Rwf**

Importantly to know is that taxes in ancient Rwanda were paid under the form of *Ikoro* as explained above. This

Ikoro was from the harvest (for farmers), fabricated products, and domestic animals or from hunting activities. Apart from *Ikoro* that was recognized as due to the King, the Chiefs and Sub-Chiefs had also right to claim from their people what was called "*Umusogongero*" and this was equivalent to 10 days manpower per year to the Sub-Chiefs and three days manpower per year to the Chiefs.[24] Starting from the 01st January 1932, *Ikoro* was translated into 0,50 Rwf per taxpayer and was paid at the same time as head tax, and was later on increased to 2 Rwf in 1953[25] while *Umusogongero* was felt into abeyance after 01st January 1932.[26]

Since colonization period and after colonization, the reasons and means of taxation progressively improved. It is in this regard that contribution in nature was replaced by taxation in terms of money. Still, the history shows that legislation on taxation came in Rwanda from the colonial regimes such as the Ordinance of August 1912 that established graduated tax and tax on real property, Ordinance of 15th November 1925 adopting and putting into application the Order issued in Belgium Congo on 01st June 1925 establishing a profit tax.

After colonization, the first tax legislation was adopted on 2nd June 1964 governing profit tax, which was repealed and replaced by the law n° 8/97 of 26/06/1997 on the code

---

[24] I. Linden, *Christianisme et pouvoirs au Rwanda (1900-1990)*, translated and revised from English by P. Geraud, Paris, Karthala, 1999, p. 244 cited in Nikozitambirwa, "De l'Impot Ikoro", available at http://users.skynet.be/wihogora/niko-rmm-ikoro-020503.htm, accessed on 15th June 2011.

[25] R. Bourgeois, *Banyarwanda et Barundi*, T. 2, Bruxelles, IRCB, 1954, n° 49, cited in Nikozitambirwa, "De l'Impot Ikoro", available at http://users.skynet.be/wihogora/niko-rmm-ikoro-020503.htm, accessed on 15th June 2011.

[26] *Ibid.*

of direct taxes on different profits and professional incomes. This code has been modified and complemented many times up to the current version.

In addition, the administration and accountability of taxes and duties in Rwanda was initially under the ministry of finance and economic planning. It is in 1997 that the Rwanda Revenue Authority (RRA) was created by the law n° 15/97 of 8/11/1997 to administer the various taxes and tax related laws and to asses, collect, administer, and account for fiscal and customs revenue collected to the government through the ministry of finance in accordance with established procedure.

II.2. Main principles governing tax in Rwanda

Under Rwandan tax law, different principles govern this field of law and most of them have a direct or indirect relationship with the ordinary general principles of law. Among those principles, some are constitutional whereas others are general principles of law and not constitutional.

II.2.1. Constitutional principles

Those are some principles that are reflected into constitutional provisions, in other words, those are the principle of tax law but which at the same time can be found in the Constitution.

II.2.1.1. The principle of legality of tax

The legality of tax constitutes a protection of the taxpayers from being subject of arbitrary taxation. This principle is provided for by article 81 of the Constitution of the Republic of Rwanda of 04th June 2003 as amended to date. This article reads, "No taxation can be imposed, modified or removed except by law. No exemption from or reduction of tax may be granted unless authorised by law".[27] This means that it is not possible to find a tax if there is no law establishing it (tax base, tax rate, tax procedure, tax sanctions, etc) and authorising its collection. In terms of article 189 of the Constitution, international agreements that commit state finances, among others, also need authorisation of the Parliament to be ratified.

In this regard, the principle of legality of tax calls mainly an intervention of the legislative power. However, the executive power has also some powers to intervene through issuance of rules and orders (regulatory power of the executive).

II.2.1.2. The principle of equality before tax

According to article 16 of the Constitution of the Republic of Rwanda of 04th June 2003 as amended to date, all human beings are equal before the law and shall enjoy, without any discrimination, equal protection of the law. This principle of equality leads to the main characteristics of law that is the general character of a law and impersonality of a law. This principle also refers to the equality before public charges, which is one of the main principles of public law. Applied to tax law, this principle means that all taxpayers must be treated equally before tax law. On this point, worthy to mention that equality of tax law is not and can never be numerical equality but rather equality based on fiscal justice where the major guiding principle is to contribute reference made to the capacity of each taxpayer.

---

[27] Art. 81 para. 1 and 2 of the Constitution of 04th June 2003 as amended to date.

II.2.1.3. The principle of liberty

This principle refers to personal liberty/freedom as well as commercial freedom or business liberty. In fact, this principle refers to the fact that any given taxpayer has full freedom to run and manage his/her business in a way he/she likes. In other words, every person is free to organise his/her business in a way that better fits his/her interests.

Due to the variety of taxes, it is not surprising for a taxpayer to fall under a given tax category and it is then up to him/her to accept or not falling under that category. This is justified by the principle of freedom of management as well as the principle of non-interference into one's business. Thus, a person can decide to make profits or not and no person can compel someone else to make profits.

However, in tax law, like in any other field of law, justice requires limitation of personal liberty as far as this liberty infringes freedoms of others. This means that the principle of freedom is recognized and protected as far as it is exploited with good faith and any abuse of freedom cannot be tolerated.

II.2.2. Non-constitutional principles

Two famous general principles of law are applicable in tax law too. Those principles are: the principle of non-retroactivity of the law and the principle of territoriality of the law.

II.2.2.1. The principle of non-retroactivity

The principle that none is presumed to be ignorant of law requires that all laws be published before coming into force. In most cases, the publication day is the same day for a law to enter into force. But sometimes, a law can be published in the Official Gazette but enter into force sometime after. This happens when the legislator deems that there is need of making it known to the public before it can be enforced.

The principle of non-retroactivity is provided for in most constitutions as well as in some civil codes.[28] The non-retroactivity of laws is dictated by the desire to maintain order and social stability. It would be in fact creating a legal insecurity to apply a new law to a past activity. Consequently, it is unquestionably accepted that laws have effect in future i.e. applicable to the situation that happened after they entered into force. However, this principle of non-retroactivity of laws itself is not absolute and accepts some limitations/exceptions. This is for instance in cases where the legislator has expressly declared a given law to be retro-active, cases of interpretative laws and cases of retroactivity in *mitius*.

Tax laws follow the similar philosophy and apply the principle of non-retroactivity and its exceptions. Thus once declared to enter into force, a tax law governs not only the future actions but also applies to ongoing situations. However, tax legislator may also declare a given tax law to be retroactive and in the same sense, tax interpretative laws are always retroactive, the same as *mitius* tax laws.

II.2.2.2. The principle of territoriality

This principle concerns the application of tax law in space. It is a general principle that laws are only applicable within the boundaries of the concerned country. In tax matter, this is referred to as tax sovereignty. However, tax authorities may in some instances tax revenues gained

---

[28] For instance art. 2 of the Rwandan Civil Code Book I.

outside the country's territory or vice-versa i.e. not to tax revenues gained within the boundaries of the country. This mainly happens in cases of tax conventions, where tax sovereignty can be violated in benefit of such international conventions. This may also happen in cases of some exceptional laws like for instance the laws establishing free zones.

This principle of territoriality has got some implications mainly issues of double taxation and tax evasion. If it is possible to avoid double taxation internally, the issue becomes very complicated internationally because there is no international order regulating double taxation except some bilateral or multilateral double taxation avoidance agreements. In fact, each State is sovereign in tax matters. Apart from the problem of double taxation, the State sovereignty in tax matters also leads to the problem of tax evasion.

II.3. Rwandan tax structure

In Rwanda, there are taxes collected by the central Government and taxes collected by the districts. Taxes that are collected by the central Government are Value Added Tax (VAT), Direct Taxes on Income such as personal income tax, corporate income tax, withholding tax, property tax on boats, registration fees for vehicles, consumption tax and import duties. Taxes that are collected by the districts are the property taxes (excluding boats), tax on rental revenues and trading licences. Taxes that are collected by the central government are referred to as centralised taxes while taxes that are collected by the districts are referred to as decentralised taxes.

II.3.1. Centralized taxes

Centralised taxes refer to taxes collected by the central government through Rwanda Revenue Authority (RRA).

RRA was created in 1997 to serve as independent public organ in charge of collecting taxes, and having that as a sole mandate of it. Since that time, the mission of tax collection was shifted from the ministry of finance to RRA.

II.3.1.1. Value Added Tax (VAT)

II.3.1.1.1. Historical background

This tax began in France in the year 1954. It reached Africa through the countries that were colonized by France such as Ivory Coast in the year 1959, Senegal in 1960 and Madagascar in 1969. It further reached other countries like Kenya in 1990, Uganda in 1996 and Tanzania in 1998. VAT was first introduced in Rwanda in January 2001 by the law n° 06/2001 of 20/01/2001.

II.3.1.1.2. VAT Registration

Under Rwandan law, there are two avenues to register for VAT: compulsory registration and voluntary registration.

Compulsory registration

Any person who carries out taxable activities exceeding twenty million Rwanda Francs (20,000,000 RWF) in the previous fiscal year, or five million Rwanda Francs (5,000,000 RWF) the preceding calendar quarter is required to register for VAT with the tax administration within a period of seven (7) days from the end of the year or from the end of the quarter mentioned above.[29]

Voluntary registration

As far as voluntary registration is concerned, the law says that any person who is not required to register for VAT

[29] Art. 10.2 of the law n° 25/2005.

may voluntarily register with the tax administration for VAT.[30]

II.3.1.1.3. VAT taxable activities

VAT is charged on transactions involving the supply of goods in Rwanda, supply of services in Rwanda and importation of the same into Rwanda. According to same article, the term supply for goods means a disposition of the goods for a consideration and supply of service mean the performance of the service for a consideration. Similarly, anything which is not a supply of goods but is done for a consideration (including: lease, hire, assignment or surrender of any right or interest) is a supply of service.[31]

II.3.1.1.4. VAT standard rate and time for payment

The standard VAT rate is 18% to all taxable goods and services.[32] As far as the time for payment is concerned, there are two regimes:

- **The period of 15 days of the subsequent month:** VAT returns are filed not later than the 15th day of the subsequent month.[33] This regime is applicable to any taxpayer whose annual turnover is above two hundred million Rwandan francs (200,000,000 Rwf).
- **The period of 15 days after the end of the quarter:** For taxpayers whose annual turnover is equal or less than two hundred million Rwandan

---

[30] *Ibid.*

[31] Art. 3 of the law n° 06/2001 of 20/01/2001.

[32] Art. 1 of the law n° 23/2002 of 10/07/2002 modifying and completing the law n°06 0f 20/01/2001 on the code of Value Added Tax.

[33] Art. 1.1 of the law n° 25/2010 of 28/05/2010 modifying and complementing law n°06/2001 of 20/01/2001 on the Code of Value Added Tax.

francs (200,000,000 Rwf), the tax declaration of VAT is quarterly and is deposited with payment of the tax due within fifteen (15) days after the end of the quarter to which the VAT is referred. However, voluntary declaration on a monthly basis by any taxpayer is admissible for VAT taxpayers whose turnover is equal or less than two hundred million Rwandan francs (200,000,000 Rwf).[34]

II.3.1.1.5. Zero rate VAT and exonerations

Zero rate is applicable to exports and supplies to privileged persons.[35] VAT exonerations[36] are provided for

---

[34] Art. 1.2 of the law n° 25/2010 of 28/05/2010 modifying and complementing the law n°06/2001 of 20/01/2001 on the code of Value Added Tax.

[35] These are:

a) Goods imported for the official purposes of a diplomatic mission accredited by the Republic of Rwanda, but only to the extent that, where there is a diplomatic mission of Rwanda in the country of the diplomat or the diplomatic mission, the foreign country grants reciprocal privileges to the diplomats and diplomatic mission, or consulates of Rwanda.

b) Supplies made under the agreement entered between the government of Rwanda and the donor(s), the supply (i) funded by the project under the agreement and (ii) provided by the donor through the Agreement, where the evidence indicate that the supply is made pursuant to the terms of the agreement, as the Commissioner General may prescribe.

c) Supplies made to the donor in Rwanda, in the course of implementing donor funded projects.

d) Supplies or importation made under technical aid Agreement, which are exempted under other laws of the country.

[36] As modified and complemented by article 2 of the law n° 25/2010 of 28/05/2010, are VAT exonerated water supply services; goods and services for health purposes; educational materials and services; books, newspapers, journals and other electronic equipments used as educational materials; transport services; lending, lease and sale (of houses); financial and insurance services; precious metals; funeral services; energy supplies ("essence" and "mazout" are not included); trade union subscriptions; leasing of exempted goods; agricultural

by article 86 of the VAT law as modified and complemented by article 2 of the law n° 25/2010 of 28/05/2010.

II.3.1.2. Direct taxes on income

The direct taxes on income in Rwanda are the personal income tax and corporate tax.

II.3.1.2.1. Personal income tax

Under Rwandan law, the taxable income as far as personal income tax is concerned is composed of the Business profits and Investment income.

II.3.1.2.1.1. Business profits

The tax base is the business profit, determined as the income from all business activities reduced by all business expenses.[37] In determining profits on business activities, expenses are deductible if (a) they are incurred for the direct purpose of, and in the normal course of the business; (b) they correspond to a real expense and can be substantiated with proper documents; (c) they lead to a decrease in the net assets of the business; and (d) they are used for activities related to the tax period in which they are incurred.

The following expenses are not deductible from taxable profits[38]: (a) cash bonuses, attendance fees and other similar payments made to the members of the Board of Directors; (b) dividends declared and paid-out profit shares; (c) interest paid on loans denominated in a

---

inputs and equipments; goods and services imported by persons with investment certificate (like raw materials and machines; equipments of information, communication and technology as they appear on annex to this law).

[37] Art. 16, 1 of the Law n° 16/2005.

[38] Art. 2 of the law n° 73/2008 of 31/12/2008.

currency other than the Rwandan Franc in excess of the London Inter-Bank Offered Rate (LIBOR) at the beginning of a tax period with an increment of one percent (1%); (d) reserve allowances, savings and other special purpose funds, unless otherwise provided for by the law; (e) fines and similar penalties; (f) donations and gifts exceeding one per cent (1%) of turnover as well as donations given to profit making persons; (g) income tax paid in accordance with this law or paid abroad on business profit and recoverable Value Added tax; (h) personal consumption expenses; and (i) entertainment expenses.

All Training and Research expenses incurred that promote activities during a tax period are considered as deductible from taxable profits.[39] In the determination of business profit, depreciation for business assets is deducted from taxable profits by the owner of those assets.[40] However, land, fine arts, antiquities, jewellery and any other assets that is not subject to wear and tear or obsolescence are not depreciated.[41] The rates for depreciation of assets are provided for by article 3 of the law n° 73/2008 of 31/12/2008.

Bad debts are also deductible. In the determination of business profit, a deduction is allowed for bad debts if the following conditions are fulfilled[42]: (a) if an amount corresponding to the debt was previously included in the income of the taxpayer; (b) if the debt is written off in the books of accounts of the taxpayer; and (c) if the taxpayer has taken all possible steps in pursuing payment and has shown concrete proofs that the debtor is insolvent.

---

[39] Art. of the law n° 16/2005.
[40] Art. 24.1 of the law n° 16/2005.
[41] Art. 24.2 of the law n° 16/2005.
[42] Art. 28.1 of the law n° 16/2005.

Banks are also allowed to deduct in the determination of business profit, any increase of the mandatory reserve for non performing loans as required by the directives related to management of bank loans and similar institutions of the National Bank of Rwanda.[43]

Still in determining the business profits, if the determination of business profit results in a loss in a tax period, the loss may be deducted from the business profit in the next five (5) tax periods, earlier losses being deducted before later losses.[44]

a) Business profit tax rate

There are two regimes as far as the rates for business taxes are concerned: the real regime and the forfeit regime.
The real regime *(Le régime réel)* is applicable to a business whose annual turnover is above 50,000,000 Rwf. In this regime, taxable income is rounded to the nearest thousand (1,000) Rwandan francs and taxed according to the following table[45]:

Annual Taxable Income (Rwf)		**Tax Rate**
From	**To**	
0	360,000	0%
360,001	1,200,000	20%
1,200,001	and greater	30%

It is important to here note that the taxable income is obtained by deducting all deductions from the total income.

---

43 Art. 4 of the law n° 73/2008 of 31/12/2008.
44 Art. 29.1 of the law n° 16/2005.
45 Art. 2.1° of the law n° 28/2012 of 27/07/2012 modifying and complementing the law n° 16/2005 on direct taxes on income as modified and complemented to date.

The forfeit regime (*Le régime forfaitaire)* distinguishes small enterprises from micro enterprises. Small enterprises pay a fixed percentage tax of 3% on annual turnover.[46] "Small Enterprises" refer to any business activity whose turnover is between twelve million and one Rwandan francs (Rwf 12.000.001) and fifty million Rwandan francs (Rwf 50.000.000) per tax period.[47] Small enterprises can renounce to the fixed percentage imposition by opting for the real regime in carrying out accounting in compliance with national accounting plan. When they opt for the real regime, they must inform the Tax Administration and this decision is irrevocable for a period of three (3) years starting from the date the Tax administration is informed. As far as the micro-enterprises[48] are concerned, they pay a flat amount of tax with reference to their annual turnover, as indicated in the following table:

Annual turnover in Rwf	**Annual flat amount of tax due in Rwf**
From 2.000.000 to 4.000.000	60,000
From 4.000.001 to 7.000.000	120,000
From 7.000.001 to 10.000.000	210,000
From 10.000.001 to 12.000.000	300,000

46 *Ibid,* art. 2.2°.

47 *Ibid,* art. 1.7°.

48 In terms of art. 1.7° of the law n° 28/2012 of 27/07/2012, micro-enterprise refers to any business activities, which result into a turnover equal to or of less than twelve million Rwandan francs (Rwf 12.000.000) per tax period;

b) Business profit tax declaration[49]

A taxpayer who receives taxable business profit prepares an annual tax declaration in accordance with the form determined by the Tax Administration and presents it, at the same time, with the accounting balance sheet, profit and loss statement for the tax period, the annexes thereto, as well as any other relevant document required by the Tax Administration, not later than 31st March of the following tax period.

The amount of tax to be paid is calculated on the basis of the annual basic declaration, reduced by (a) the tax withheld before, in accordance with Article 51 and 52 of the Law n° 16/2005 of 18/08/2005 on direct taxes on income (these are mainly the Withholding Tax on Imports and Public Tenders); and (b) the quarterly prepayments made during the tax period as mentioned above.

The tax is paid to the Tax Administration on the same day as the presentation of the annual tax declaration. A withholding or prepayment that exceeds the amount of tax liability is considered by the tax administration as liquidation of tax arrears or as the payment of any future tax obligations. Upon a written request by the taxpayer and upon satisfaction that prior tax obligations have been discharged, the Tax Administration returns to the taxpayer the excess amount within thirty (30) days from the date of receipt of the request.

c) Quarterly prepayments[50]

During the current tax period, the taxpayer pays to the account of the Tax Administration before and not later than June 30th, September 30th and December 31st of the year of taxable activities each twenty five (25%) per cent

[49] Art. 6 and 2 of the law n° 73/2008 of 31/12/2008.

[50] Art. 5 of the law n°73/2008 of 31/12/2008.

of the tax liability as calculated in the tax declaration of the previous tax period. The amount to be paid is reduced by the tax withheld in that tax period in accordance with articles 51 and 52 of the law n° 16/2005 of 18/08/2005 on direct taxes on income (these are mainly the Withholding Tax on Imports and Public Tenders).

It is important to note that income derived from agricultural activities is exempt, if the proceeds from these activities do not exceed twelve million (12,000,000) Rwandan francs in tax period.[51]

II.3.1.2.1.2. Investment income

Income derived from investment includes any payments in cash or in kind by an individual in the form of interest, dividend, royalty, or rent[52] that has not been taxed as business income.[53]

a. Interest incomes

Interest income is subject to a flat tax of fifteen percent (15%).[54] Interest income includes income from loans, deposits, guarantees, and current accounts. It also includes income from government securities, income from bonds, and negotiable securities issued by public and private companies income from cash bonds.[55] If payment of interest was subject to reduction of withholding tax as stipulated in article 51 of the law no 16/2005, the taxpayer shall not pay this tax.[56]

---

[51] Art. 18 and 33.2 of the law n° 16/2005.

[52] This "rent" should not be confused with the "tax on rental income" which has been decentralized to the districts, see infra.

[53] Art. 32 of the law n° 16/2005.

[54] Art. 33.1 of the law n° 16/2005.

[55] Art. 33.3 of the law n° 16/2005.

[56] Art. 33.2 of the law n° 16/2005.

b. Dividend Income

Dividend income is subject to a flat tax of fifteen percent (15%).[57] If dividend distribution was subject to withholding tax as stipulated in Article 51 of the law no 16/2005, the taxpayer does not pay this tax[58]. Dividend income includes income from shares and similar income distributed by companies.[59]

c. Royalty Income

The term "royalty income" includes all payments of any kind received as a prize for the use of, or the right to use, any copyright of literary, craftsmanship or scientific work including cinematograph films, films, or tapes used for radio or television broadcasting. The term also includes any payment received from using a trademark, design or model, computer application and plan secret formula or process. It also includes the price of using, or of the right to use industrial, commercial or scientific equipment or for information concerning industrial, commercial or scientific or experience. Royalty income includes also natural resource payments.[60]

Royalty income is subject to a flat tax of fifteen percent (15%).[61] If a royalty payment is subject to withholding tax as stipulated in article 51, the taxpayer does not pay this tax on royalty income.[62]

d. Rental Income

All revenues derived from rent of machinery and other equipment and land including livestock in Rwanda, are

---

[57] Art. 34.1 of the law n° 16/2005.
[58] Art. 34.2 of the law n° 16/2005.
[59] Art. 34.3 of the law n° 16/2005.
[60] Art. 35.3 of the law n° 16/2005.
[61] Art. 35.1 of the law n° 16/2005.
[62] Art. 35.2 of the law n° 16/2005.

included in taxable income, reduced by[63] ten percent (10%) of gross revenue as deemed expense; interest paid on loans; and depreciation expenses.

II.3.1.2.2. Corporate Income Tax

The following entities are subject to corporate income tax:[64] companies established in accordance with Rwandan law or foreign law; cooperative societies and their branches; public business enterprises; partnerships; entities established by Districts, Towns and Municipalities and the City of Kigali, to the extent that these entities conduct business; *de facto* companies or associations and any other entities that perform business activities, and are established to realize profits.

The Government of Rwanda and the following entities are exempted from corporate income tax:[65] the City of Kigali, Districts, Towns and Municipalities; the National Bank of Rwanda; entities that carry on only activities of a religious, humanitarian, charitable, scientific or educational character, unless the revenue received during a tax period exceeds the corresponding expenses or to the extent that those entities conduct a business; international organizations, agencies of technical cooperation and their representatives, if such exemption is provided for by international agreements; qualified pension funds; the Rwanda Social Security Fund; and the Rwanda Development Bank.

---

[63] Art. 36.1 of the law n° 16/2005.
[64] Art. 38.1 of the law n° 16/2005.
[65] Art. 39 of the law n° 16/2005.

a) Corporate Tax rate

Taxable Business profit is rounded down to the nearest 1,000 RWF and taxed at a rate of thirty percent (30%).[66] However, a registered investment entity that operates in a Free Trade Zone and foreign companies that have their headquarters in Rwanda that fulfils the requirements stipulated in the Rwandan law on Investment Promotion are entitled to pay corporate income tax at the rate of zero per cent (0%).[67]

b) Tax Declaration

A taxpayer who receives taxable business profit prepares an annual tax declaration in accordance with the form determined by the tax administration and presents it, at the same time, with the accounting balance sheet, profit and loss statement for the tax period, the annexes thereto, as well as any other relevant document required by the Tax Administration, not later than 30th day of the sixth month of the following tax period.[68]

c) Quarterly prepayments[69]

During the current tax period, the taxpayer pays to the account of the Tax Administration before and not later than June 30th, September 30th and December 31st of the year of taxable activities each twenty five (25%) per cent of the tax liability as calculated in the tax declaration of the previous tax period. The final amount of tax to be paid is calculated on the basis of the annual basic declaration, reduced by the prepayments.[70]

---

[66] Art. 41.1 of the law n° 16/2005.
[67] Art. 41.2 of the law n° 16/2005.
[68] Art. 43.1 of the law n° 16/2005.
[69] Art. 5 of the law n° 73/2008 of 31/12/2008.
[70] Art. 43.2 of the law n° 16/2005.

Important to note is that corporate taxable profit is calculated in accordance with the principles applied when calculating profits on individual businesses.[71]

II.3.1.2.3. Withholding taxes

Withholding taxes are classified into three: withholding taxes on employment incomes (referred to as pay as you earn tax), withholding taxes on imports and public tenders and withholding taxes on other payments.

A withholding agent who fails to withhold tax in accordance with the law is personally liable to pay to the Tax Administration the amount of tax that has not been withheld including penalties and interest on arrears. However, the agent is entitled to recover this amount from the payee excluding the associated fines and the interest on arrears.[72]

II.3.1.2.3.1. Pay as You Earn (PAYE) tax

This is the tax on employment income (*Taxe Professionnelle sur les Remunerations*). The persons who are obliged to withhold and pay tax on employment income are[73] (a) an individual or an entity that pays its employees in cash or benefits in kind and (b) an entity that pays out pensions excluding pensions paid according to procedures of the State Social Security.

Employment income includes all payments paid to an employee in cash or in kind such as[74] (a) wages, salary, leave pay, sick pay and medical allowance, payment in lieu of leave, fees, commissions, bonuses including gratuity and incentives; (b) allowances, including any cost

[71] Art. 44 of the law n° 16/2005.
[72] Art. 53 of the law n° 16/2005.
[73] Art. 48.1 of the law n° 16/2005.
[74] Art. 13 of the law n° 16/2005.

of living, subsistence, rent, and entertainment or travel allowance; (c) any discharge or reimbursement of expenses incurred by the employee or an associate; (d) payments to the employee for his or her acceptance to work in any conditions of employment; (e) payments for redundancy or loss or termination; (f) pension payments, except those paid by the Social Security Fund of Rwanda, which are exonerated (art. 48, 2 Law n° 16/2005) and (g) other payments made in respect of current, previous or future employment.

Benefits in kind received by an employee are also included in taxable income in consideration of market value as follows:[75]

- there shall be added to the taxable income an amount meant for the availability and use of a motor vehicle to an employee during a tax period, valued at ten percent (10%) of the employment income excluding benefits in kind;
- income on a loan including advance on a salary exceeding a three (3) months salary given to an employee is valued at a difference between:
    - the interest on loan, which would have been paid by the employee during the month in which the loan was received, calculated at a rate of interest offered to commercial banks by the National Bank of Rwanda;
    - the actual interest paid by the employee in that month;
- There shall be added to the taxable income an amount meant for use or availability for use of premises including or excluding any household equipment of other contents by an employer for residential occupation by an employee during a tax

[75] Art. 15 of the law n° 16/2005.

period, valued at twenty percent (20%) of the employment income excluding benefits in kind;

- Benefits provided by an employer to a person related to an employee when there is no service rendered, are treated as if provided to the employee;
- Benefits provided by a company to one of its members are considered in the same manner as benefits an employer gives to an employee.

a) Tax declaration

An employer that is subject to withholding tax must, within fifteen (15) days following the end of each month[76], (a) file a tax declaration through procedures specified by the Commissioner General and transmit the tax withheld to the tax administration; and (b) transmit to the employee a statement indicating his/her name, the amount and type of income and the amount of tax withheld and paid.

b) Pay as you earn rate

Monthly employment income, which includes the amount an employee is paid on an extra ordinary basis as well as the bonus and the benefits he or she receives in kind, is subject to tax in accordance with the rate as shown in the table below:[77]

Monthly Taxable Income (Rwf)		Tax Rate
From	**To**	
0	30,000	0%
30,001	100,000	20%
100,001	and greater	30%

[76] Art. 48.3 of the law n° 16/2005.

[77] Art. 50.1 of the law n° 16/2005.

c) Casual labourers

Income from a casual labourer is subject to tax at a special rate of fifteen percent (15%). However, in computing casual labourer's tax, an income not exceeding thirty thousand (30,000 Rwf) per month is rated at zero percent (0%).[78] Under Rwandan law, "Casual labourer" means an employee or worker who performs unskilled labour activities, who does not use machinery or equipment requiring special skills, and who is engaged by an employer for an aggregate period not exceeding thirty (30) days during a tax period.[79]

d) Second employment

An employer who is not the first employer of a taxpayer is required to withhold tax at market at the top marginal rate of 30%[80]. According to article 2, 2^0 of Law no 16/2005, "first employer" means an employer who gives greater annual income to an employee by comparison with another employer. It is therefore this "other employer" who must be understood as "second employer".

II.3.1.2.3.2. Withholding Tax on Imports and public Tenders

A withholding tax of five percent (5%) of the value of goods imported for commercial use shall be paid at custom on the CIF (cost insurance and freight value) value before the goods are released by customs.[81]

A withholding tax of three percent (3%) on the sum of invoice, excluding the value added tax, is retained on payments by public institutions to those who supply goods and services based on public tenders.[82] The following

[78] Art. 50.2 of the law n° 16/2005.
[79] Art. 2 of the law n° 16/2005.
[80] Art. 48.4 of the law n° 16/2005.
[81] Art. 52.1 of the law n° 16/2005.
[82] Art. 52.2 of the law n° 16/2005.

taxpayers are exempted from withholding tax mentioned above:[83] (a) those whose business profit is exempt from taxation and (b) those who have tax clearance certificate issued by the Commissioner General of Rwanda Revenue Authority.

The Commissioner General of Rwanda Revenue Authority issues a tax clearance certificate to taxpayers who have filed their tax declarations on their business activities; paid the tax due on a regular basis, and have no tax arrears. The certificate is valid in the year in which it was issued.[84]

II.3.1.2.3.3. Withholding Tax on other payments

A withholding tax of fifteen (15%) percent is levied on the following payments made by resident individuals or resident entities including tax-exempt entities[85]: dividends, (except those governed by Article 45 of the income tax law); interests; royalties; service fees including management and technical service fees; performance payments made to an artist, a musician or an athlete irrespective of whether paid directly or through an entity that is not resident in Rwanda; lottery and other gambling proceeds.

II.3.1.2.4. Property tax: 4th base: boats

Earlier, Property tax was based on 6 bases of which the 5th and 3rd bases were abrogated while base 1, 2, and 6 are decentralized to the districts. The property tax, which is collected by the Government, is therefore based on only one base, which is the 4th base, namely tax on boats.
This tax is due by natural or juristic persons who own boats in Rwanda. It is not due for boats that are used by persons who have no domicile, residence or permanent

[83] Art. 52.3 of the law n° 16/2005.
[84] Art. 52.4 of the law n° 16/2005.
[85] Art. 51.1 of the law n° 16/2005.

establishment in Rwanda.[86] The property tax on boat is governed by the Law-Decree of 28/12/1973, related to the property tax, in Official Gazette n° 7/74.

II.3.1.2.5. Registration fees for vehicles

Any imported car must pay registration fee to get a plate number. The same fees are paid by a car already existing in Rwanda but without a Rwandan plate number to get it. Registration fees for imported motor vehicles are determined on the basis of engine capacity as follows:[87]

Engine power (cc)		**Fees (Rwf)**
Between	**And**	
0	1,000	75,000
1,001	1,500	160,000
1,501	3,000	250,000
3,001	4,500	450,000
4,501	and above	560,000
Special vehicle		640,000

The above fees are the standard registration fees. For motor vehicles with personalized number plates registration fees is fixed at two million Rwandan francs (2,000,000 Rwf).[88]

II.3.1.2.6. Consumption taxes (Excise Taxes)

Excise duties are charged on certain goods, imported as well as locally manufactured, following the tariff provided for in article 1 of the law n° 19/2009 of 30/06/2009 modifying and completing the law n° 26/2006 of

[86] Art. 20 of the Decree Law of 28/12/1973.

[87] Art. 2 of the Ministerial Order n° 008/2009 of 01/12/2009 determining the amount of registration fees for imported and already registered vehicles in Rwanda.

[88] Art. 4 of the Ministerial Order n° 008/2009 of 01/12/2009.

27/05/2006 determining and establishing consumption tax on some imported and locally manufactured products.[89]
The following table provides some examples of consumption tax rates in Rwanda:

Products	**Tax Rate**
Fruit juices	5%
Limonade, Soda and other juices	39%
Mineral water	10%
Beer	60%
Wine	70%
Brandies, liquors and whisky	70%
Cigarettes	150%
Lubricants	37%
Vehicles with an engine capacity of less 1500 cc	5%
Vehicles with engine capacity between 1500 cc and 2500 cc	10%
Vehicles with engine capacity above 2500	15%
Powered milk	10%
Telephone communications	8%

II.3.1.2.7. Import Duties

Import duties are determined by the East African Community Customs Management Act of 2004[90], the Protocol on the Establishment of the East African Customs

[89] Art. 1 of the law n° 19/2009 of 30/06/2009 modifying and completing the law n° 26/2006 of 27/05/2006 determining and establishing consumption tax on some imported and locally manufactured products.
[90] See Section 11.

Union[91], the East African Community Rules of Origin specified in Annex III to the Protocol[92] and the Common Market External Tariff. Briefly, EAC Partner States have established a three band common external tariff with a minimum rate of 0 %, a middle rate of 10 % and a maximum rate of 25 % in respect of all products imported into the Community.[93]

II.3.2. Decentralized taxes

In its policy of allowing the population a greater role in public management, the Government of Rwanda has decentralized some powers to the local entities. It is in this egard that the following taxes have been decentralized to the districts: Property tax: 1st, 2nd and 6th bases, tax on rental revenues and trading Licence Tax (*La Patente*).

II.3.2.1. Property tax

This tax is applicable on the 1st base on occupied houses, which are registered in the land registry, the 2nd base that is on area of unused registered or unregistered plots as well as on 6th base, which is on mineral concessions.

II.3.2.1.1. 1st base: Registered occupied houses

This tax is levied on the value of houses and buildings registered in the land registry and for which the owner has obtained a title deed, from the time the house is finished, inhabited or used for any other activity.[94]

The tax is calculated on the value of the house or the building that has been declared by the taxpayer. The value

---

[91] Especially, see article 12.
[92] See art. 14 of the Protocol.
[93] Art. 12 of the Protocol.
[94] Art. 5 (a) of the law n° 17/2002 of 10/05/2002 establishing the source of revenue for districts and towns and its management, modified and complemented by the law n° 33/2003 of 06/09/2003.

of the building is determined by the District or Town Council, basing on the nature of the asset, its location and what it is meant for. Where necessary, the District or Town in which the taxable asset is located shall make a counter-evaluation of the declared value with the help of experts approved by the District or Town Council.[95]

The District or Town Council fixes the tax rate of between 0.1% and 0.2% of the determined value.[96] The tax is calculated on a year basis[97] and is due not later than March, 31st of the fiscal year.[98] The fixed asset tax is paid by the owner, possessor or usufructuary.[99]

The following houses or buildings owned with title deeds are exempted: houses or buildings intended for medical purposes, caring for vulnerable groups and those meant for educational purposes where no profit making activity takes place; houses or buildings intended only for scientific or professional activities if not meant for profit making; houses or government buildings, province/city of Kigali, districts or towns as well as public establishments except where they were built for commercial purposes; houses or buildings used for religious activities recognised by the law, with exception of those houses used for profit making purposes; houses or buildings belonging to foreign diplomatic missions in Rwanda if their countries do not levy tax on houses or buildings of Rwanda's diplomatic mission.

---

95 Art. 6 of the law n° 17/2002 of 10/05/2002 modified and complemented by the law n° 33/2003 of 06/09/2003.
96 Art. 14 of the law n° 17/2002 of 10/05/2002 modified and complemented by the law n° 33/2003 of 06/09/2003.
97 Art. 8 of the law n° 17/2002 of 10/05/2002.
98 Art. 28.1 of the law n° 17/2002 of 10/05/2002.
99 Art. 7 of the law n° 17/2002 of 10/05/2002.

II.3.2.1.2. 2nd base: Area of unbuilt plots

Tax on unbuilt registered or unregistered plots whether being subject to a long-term bail contract, rental contract or leased is calculated on the basis of square meters. That taxable surface is obtained by subtracting two times the area covered by houses from the total area of the whole concerned land.[100]

Tax on un-built plots is fixed by the District or Town Council as follows:[101]

- From twenty francs (20 Rwf) to fifty francs (50 Rwf) per square metre in the city of Kigali, fractions of square metre are not included in the calculations;
- From ten francs (10 Rwf) to twenty francs (20 Rwf) per square metre in other towns, fractions of square metre are not included in the calculations;
- In trading centre from one franc (1 Rwf) to ten francs (10 Rwf) per square metre, fractions of square metre are not included in the calculations;
- In rural areas, tax on unbuilt land shall be determined by the district or town council but shall not exceed one thousand francs (1000 Rwf) per hectare. Where the taxpayer owns more than twenty hectares (20 ha), he or she will be taxed in a lump sum ranging from one thousand and one francs (1001 Rwf) to two thousand francs (2000 Rwf) for each additional hectare on 200 ha. The first five (5) hectares are exempted from tax, and fractions of hectare shall not be considered.

According to article 17.2 of the law n° 17/2002 of 10/05/2002 as modified and complemented by the Law n°

---

[100] Art. 16 of the law n° 17/2002 of 10/05/2002.
[101] Art. 17 of the law n° 17/2002 of 10/05/2002.

33/2003 of 06/09/2003, where the unbuilt land is a tourist site, the tax shall be increased by 10% of the annual ordinary tax.

The tax is due not later than 31st March of the fiscal year.[102] The following unbuilt land is exempted from the fixed asset tax:[103] (a) land that is exclusively used for educational, medical, research and sporting activities that are proved not to be profit driven; (b) and on which government, district and town infrastructures are effected or are to be effected; (c) land used by diplomatic missions in Rwanda if their countries do not levy tax on land used by Rwanda's diplomatic missions; and (d) land used for charitable activities.

II.3.2.1.3. 6th base: Mineral concessions

Tax on land reserved for minerals prospecting and mining or quarry purposes (*exploitation des carrieres*) is calculated per square meter. This tax is paid by those who are given the right to mine or prospect for minerals or quarries.[104] Tax on an area offered for prospecting, mining or quarry is determined by the District or Town Council as follows:[105]

- the area offered for mining is taxed at a rate ranging from 2.5 Frw to 5 Frw per square meter;
- the area offered only for prospecting one type or many types of minerals is taxed at a rate ranging from 2.5 FRW to 3 FRW per square meter;
- the area offered for quarry mining (*exploitation des carrieres*) from 1 FRW up to 2 FRW per square meter.

---

[102] Art. 28.1 of the law n° 17/2002 of 10/05/2002 as modified and complemented by the Law n° 33/2003 of 06/09/2003.
[103] Art. 18 of the law n° 17/2002 of 10/05/2002.
[104] Art. 19 of the law n° 17/2002 of 10/05/2002.
[105] Art. 20 of the law n° 17/2002 of 10/05/2002.

In case the Government, parastatals carry these activities, they are exempted from that tax.[106]

II.3.2.2. Tax on rental revenues

This tax is charged on income from renting houses located in Rwanda irrespective of the country of their beneficiaries' residence or home.[107] The net profit is the difference between receipts and expenses related to rented assets.[108] The net revenue is obtained after deducting from the gross revenue expenses incurred by the owner for maintenance amounting to 70% of the gross revenue.[109]

In case the taxpayer produces proof for having paid bank interests in the same year in which the rent started and on a loan aimed at building, purchasing or maintaining taxable items, the net revenue shall be obtained by deducting from gross revenue expenses incurred on rented materials which amount to 50% of gross revenue plus interests for the banks.[110]

The District or Town's Council fixes the tax rates, which cannot go beyond the following limits:[111]

---

[106] Art. 21 of the law n° 17/2002 of 10/05/2002.
[107] Art. 54 and 55 of the law n° 17/2002 of 10/05/2002. Note that with the coming into existence of the law n° 16/2005 of 18/08/2005 on direct taxes, revenue from renting land and agricultural machines are now categorized as "investment incomes" and collected by the government. The content of article 55 should therefore be read together with this latest law.
[108] Art. 59 of the law n° 17/2002 of 10/05/2002.
[109] Art. 57.1 of the law n° 17/2002 of 10/05/2002.
[110] Art. 57.2 of the law n° 17/2002 of 10/05/2002,
[111] Art. 61 of the law n° 17/2002 of 10/05/2002.

From	To	Rate
0 frw	60,000 frw	0%
60,001 frw	180,000 frw	10 %
180,001 frw	300,000 frw	15%
300,001 frw	600,000 frw	20%
600,001frw	1,000,000 frw	25%
more than 1,000,000 frw	-	30%

The tax is payable not later than 31st March of the subsequent year.[112] Are exempted from this tax[113] the buildings and houses belonging to the State, Districts and other public entities, except those which pursue a commercial activity as well as revenues from renting houses and buildings that forms part of a "corporate income" and taxable as such.

II.3.2.3. Trading Licence Tax

Trading licence tax, commonly referred to as "*patente*" is a tax that must be paid by any natural or legal person who has decided to undertake business activities. The tax must be paid in full before starting the activity for which it is paid. The tax is determined according to where the taxpayer is operating or to the place of his/her usual residence.[114]

If the taxable activity starts in January, the trading licence tax must be paid for a whole year. If it starts after January, the taxpayer must pay tax equivalent to the remaining months including the one in which the activity started. However, as regards seasonable activities a whole year's tax must be paid, even if the taxed activities did not last for the whole year.[115] For subsequent years (i.e. for already existing business), the trading licence tax is payable not later than 31st March.[116] Trading Licence Tax

[112] Art. 61 of the law n° 17/2002 of 10/05/2002.
[113] Art. 60.2 of the law n° 17/2002 of 10/05/2002.
[114] Art. 44 of the law n° 17/2002 of 10/05/2002.
[115] Art. 48 of the law n° 17/2002 of 10/05/2002.
[116] Art. 49 of the law n° 17/2002 of 10/05/2002.

is determined from the basic licence “P” which may vary according to the type of activity and location. The basic Trading Licence Tax is fixed each year by the Council of the District or Town where taxpayers are based but does not exceed two thousand Rwanda Francs (2,000 Rwf).[117]

Trading licence is charged as indicated in the following table:[118]

Type of activity	**Rural area**	**Towns**	**Kigali City**
Vendors without shops, small scale technicians who do not use machines, transporters of people and property on motorcycles	1P	2P	2P
Traders and technicians who use machines	5P	10P	10P
Any transportation other than using motocycles	10P per Vehicle	10P per Vehicle	10P per Vehicle
Hotel business self-employed	5P	30P	100P
Professional taxpayer services rendered to others and the like	10P	20P	20P
Industries	80P	100P	120P
Imports and exports	120P	120P	120P
Insurance, banking and the like	30P	100P	100P

[117] Art. 46 of the law n° 17/2002 of 10/05/2002.

[118] Art. 47 of the law n° 17/2002 of 10/05/2002 as modified and complemented by Art. 17 of the Law n° 33/2003 of 06/09/2003.

The District or Town Administration where taxable items are located issues a trading licence certificate showing that the tax has been paid.[119] If the certificate is lost or damaged, its duplicate is issued by the competent authority at a price fixed by the District or Town Council. However, this amount cannot exceed one thousand Francs (1,000 Rwf).[120]

The trading licence certificate must be displayed clearly at the entrance of the business premises or stuck on the car for which the tax was paid. The certificate bearer must always be able to present his or her identity and function if requested by competent authority. Failure to bear or display the trading licence certificate where it's due, is punishable by a fine of five thousand Rwanda Francs (5,000 Rwf).[121]

In case the taxpayer terminates or changes his or her activities, he or she is refunded the balance on the tax already paid if there is any, depending on the remaining months to the end of December 31th of that year, provided he or she has complied with all-the laws governing other District or Town taxes.[122]

If a taxpayer fails to pay all or part of the tax, the Tax Collector of the District or Town or any other authorised staff, after submitting the related report, may confiscate the concerned goods and immediately suspend the taxpayer's business until he pays the tax.[123]

---

119 Art. 50 of the law n° 17/2002 of 10/05/2002 as modified and complemented by the law n° 33/2003 of 06/09/2003.
120 *Idem*, art. 52.2.
121 *Idem*, art. 51.
122 *Idem,* art. 52.1.
123 *Idem,* art. 53.2.

Are exempted from paying trading licence[124] the Government of Rwanda, its provinces and districts and towns when they carry out non-profit making activities; corporate persons and organisations that are exempted from paying corporate tax in accordance with article 5 of the law on the code of direct taxes on various profits and professional income; and natural or corporate persons who are engaged in agricultural or livestock activities.

II.4. Tax incentives under Rwandan law

Tax incentive is a generic term for all the measures adopted by the government to deliberately manipulate the tax system to the advantage of a potential taxpayer.[125] In other words, tax incentive refers to a deliberate reduction in or total elimination of tax liability granted by the government in order to encourage a particular economic unit to act in some desirable ways, which may be to invest more, produce more, employ more, export more, sell more, consume less, import less and pollute less.[126] Under Rwandan law, different tax incentives are available and are granted upon fulfilment of the required conditions.

II.4.1. Profit tax discount

Under Rwandan tax law, examples of profit tax discount include cases of employment of a large number of Rwandans as well as the cases of exports that bring in Rwanda high amount of incomes.

According to article 41 of Income tax law, an investor is entitled to a profit tax discount on different rates

---

[124] *Idem,* art. 45.

[125] P. Dotun, "Corporate Tax Incentives and Economic Growth in Nigeria", *Tax News*, 1996, vol. 2, n° 1.

[126] J. Olabisi, "Tax Incentive as a Catalyst for Economic Development in Nigeria", *JORIND,* December 2009, vol. 2, n° 2, p. 116.

depending on how much he/she employs Rwandan citizens. Four bands exist to this regard: a profit tax discount of 2% is granted to an investor who employs between 100 and 200 Rwandans, 5% to an investor who employs between 201 and 400 Rwandans, 6% to an investor who employs between 401 and 900 Rwandans, and 7% to an investor who employs more than 900 Rwandans.[127] Apart from the number, there exist two other conditions to benefit discount on profit tax. The first condition is to maintain the employees for a period of at least six months during a tax period whereas the second condition is about the remuneration of considered employees that must be paid an amount that is not taxed at 0%.[128]

Another category of profit tax discount is granted to an investor taxpayer who exports commodities or services that bring to the country a large amount of incomes. If the exported commodities or services bring to the country between 3,000,000 USD and 5,000,000 USD, the taxpayer is entitled to a tax discount of 3% whereas if the exported commodities or services bring to the country more than 5,000,000 USD the tax discount becomes 5%.[129]

II.4.2. Investment allowance

According to the law n° 16/2005 of 18/08/2005 on direct taxes on income, an investment allowance of 40% of the invested amount in new or used assets maybe depreciated excluding motor vehicles that carry less than 8 persons,

---

127 Art. 41 of the law n° 16/2005 of 18/08/2005 on direct taxes on income as modified and completed by the law n° 73/2008 of 31/12/2008 modifying and complementing the law n° 16/2005 of 18/08/2005 on direct taxes on income in *O.G.* n° 19 of 11/05/2009, hereinafter referred to as Income Tax Law.

128 Art. 41 *in fine* of the Income tax law.

129 Art. 42 of the Income tax law.

except those exclusively used in a tourist business, is deductible for a registered investor in the first tax period of purchase and/or of use of such an asset if the conditions provided for by the law are fulfilled.[130]

The investment allowance becomes 50% instead of 40% if the registered business is located outside Kigali or falls within the priority sectors determined by the Investment Code of Rwanda.[131]

II.4.3. Research and development tax incentives

Under Rwandan tax law, research and development tax incentives are provided for by article 27 of the law on income tax according to which all training and research expenses incurred and declared as agreed by a taxpayer and which promote activities during a tax period are considered as deductible from taxable profits.

II.4.4. Tax holidays

Under a tax holiday, qualifying newly established firms are not required to pay corporate income tax for a specified time period, in order to encourage investment.[132] Thus, tax holidays refer to temporary exemption of a new firm or investment from certain specified taxes, typically at least corporate income tax, sometimes the waiver of administrative requirements notably the need to file tax returns.[133] Under Rwandan law, an example of tax

---

[130] Art. 26 of the Income tax law. Such conditions are cumulative and are as follows: (a) the amount of business assets invested is equal to 30,000,000 Rwandan francs, and (b) the business assets are held at the establishment for at least three (3) tax periods after the tax period in which the investment allowance was taken into consideration.

[131] Art. 26 par. 2 of the Income tax law.

[132] W. S. Clark, "Tax Incentives for Foreign Direct Investment: Empirical Evidence on Effects and Alternative Policy Options", *Canadian Tax Journal*, vol. 48, nº 4, 2000, p. 1145.

[133] A. Klemm, *op. cit.*, p. 4.

holidays can be found in article 42 paragraph 3 of the law on income tax, in terms of which, companies that carry out micro-finance activities approved by competent authorities pay corporate income tax at the rate of 0% for a period of five (5) years from the time of the approval of the activity, with a possibility for this period to be renewed by the order of the Minister.

II.4.5. Tax incentives in Special Economic Zones

Under Rwandan law, special economic zones are governed by the law n° 05/2011 of 21/03/2011 regulating special economic zones in Rwanda.[134] This law whose purpose is the establishment, development, operation and maintenance of SEZs in Rwanda, doesn't define what a special economic zone is.

According to the same law, parties or stakeholders to a SEZ are three namely:

Developer: an individual or a legal entity, which holds a licence for establishing and developing a zone or a part of a zone in accordance with the laws and relevant regulations. To establish a zone, an interested individual or legal entity applies to the Special Economic Zone Regulatory Authority (SEZAR) that grants it. A Zone maybe established on any land, being private or public, provided that the appropriate procedures with regard to sale, expropriation, etc are respected.

Operator: an individual or legal entity that is licensed to operate a zone according to the relevant laws and under the terms of the Zone Operator Agreement with SEZAR.

[134] In *O.G.* n° special of 30 March 2011.

User: an individual or legal entity that is licensed to carry out activities in part or the entire Zone according to the relevant laws and under the terms of an agreement with a Zone Operator and the SEZAR. The User is not allowed to carry out activity that is on the negative list and the User license may be transferred subject to approval by SEZAR. The requirements for a Zone user applicant are set for in article 26 of the SEZ law.

A Zone developer or operator is entitled to dispose of the land of the area within the limits of the establishment decision.[135] He/she also has right to freely set prices for land and fees for service delivery in the area depending on invested capital and expected profits, unless otherwise determined in the establishment decision. He/she can also mortgage such land. To become a Zone developer or operator, the applicant must be a legal entity incorporated and established in Rwanda and demonstrate financial and technical capability.

According to article 33 and the following articles of the law on Special Economic Law, imported goods shall enter Free Trade Zone (FTZ) areas free from customs duties, and Duty-free goods may remain in storage in FTZ areas for a time as specified in the regulations for the Zone. Foreign merchandise brought into a FTZ area may also be repacked, assembled, distributed, sorted, graded, cleaned, mixed with domestic or foreign merchandises. If such merchandise are sold outside the Custom Territory (outside East African Community), they shall be considered to be imported, produced, or manufactured outside the Customs Territory and shall be duty-free. However, if such merchandises are sold in the Customs Territory, they shall be subject to the relevant duties

[135] Art. 24 of the SEZ law.

determined by the customs regulations. Unless otherwise provided for by the law, Zone developers, operators and users are bound to comply with tax laws in force in Rwanda.

II.5. Tax procedure and tax litigation in Rwanda

The tax procedures are reflected by the duties of a taxpayer (also referred to as fiscal obligations) that result into different procedures to be followed by the taxpayer.

II.5.1. The taxpayers' duties

Under Rwandan law, a taxpayer has different duties like a duty to file tax return, duty to pay due tax, and some other particular duties.

II.5.1.1. Filing tax returns

Filing tax returns is also referred to as filing tax decalartion. Like in other countries, the determination of the payable tax is made in the first degree by the taxpayer him/herself by way of declaration. In the second degree, the declaration filed by the taxpayer is verified by the Fiscal Administration. The taxpayer is obliged to file a declaration even when no profit was made during the taxable period. Are only allowed not to file a declaration those who are "exempted" by any relevant tax law. Declaration is made by completing a form prepared by the Fiscal Administration and these forms differ depending on the concerned type of tax.

II.5.1.1.1. Rectification

When the Tax Administration discovers a miscalculation, an omission, a misrepresentation, an understatement of income or any other error in the tax declaration or an assessment, it has the right to issue an adjusted assessment.[136] In this case, the Tax Administration (Rwanda Revenue Authority) sends a "rectification note" to the taxpayer.

The rectification note contains a draft of the adjusted assessment and all the elements leading to the adjusted assessment. It also contains penalties determined by the Tax Administration in case of non-compliance with the tax laws.[137]

The taxpayer has the right to give his or her written opinion on the rectification note within thirty (30) days. The taxpayer may also transmit additional evidence or information to indicate that the adjusted assessment is incorrect. The taxpayer has the right to a hearing on condition that he or she requested for it in his or her reply.[138] The rectification note may be issued in a period of ten (10) years, starting from 01st January, following the tax period.[139]

II.5.1.1.2. Audit and investigations

The Tax Administration may carry out audit and investigation on ground if it deems it necessary. The Tax Administration may audit a taxpayer only once in respect of a certain tax or in a certain taxable period. A new audit may be necessary if there are concrete reasons as set out

---

[136] Art. 26 of the law n° 25/2005.

[137] Art. 7 of the law n° 01/2012 of 03/02/2012 modifying and complementing law n° 25/2005 of 04/12/2005 on tax procedures as modified and complemented to date, in *O.G.* n° 13 of 26/03/2012.

[138] Art. 3 of the law n° 74/2008 of 31/12/2008 modifying and complementing law n° 25/2005 of 04/12/2005 on tax procedures.

[139] Art. 7 parag. 3 of the law n° 01/2012 of 03/02/2012 modifying and complementing law n° 25/2005 of 04/12/2005 on tax procedures as modified and complemented to date, in *O.G.* n° 13 of 26/03/2012.

by rules issued by the Commissioner General of Rwanda Revenue Authority.[140]

In case of audit, the Tax Administration is required to inform in writing ("*Avis de verification*"), the taxpayer the following:[141] (a) that he or she will be audited at least seven (7) days before the audit is conducted. If the taxpayer is not ready in seven (7) days, he writes to the tax administration requesting for an extension. This extension should not exceed fifteen (15) days and can only be allowed once; (b) the place where the audit is to be conducted and the possible duration of the audit; (c) any specific document the tax administration wants to see or any specific information it requires.

In case of audit, the taxpayer is required to receive the tax audit team by[142] (a) providing the team with suitable working premises and (b) providing the team with books and documents referred to in articles 12, 13 and 15 of Law n° 25/2005 of 04/12/2005 on Tax Procedures.

A taxpayer shall not be allowed to provide at any stage of appeal, any additional evidence that had not been produced during the audit. The preceding paragraph shall not apply in cases where the taxpayer has reasonable grounds justifying his/her inability to provide the required evidence during the audit period.[143] In case of a refund

---

[140] Art. 21 of the law n° 25/2005.

[141] Art. 20.1 of the law n° 25/2005 as modified by article 1 of the law n° 74/2008 of 31/12/2008 modifying and complementing law n° 25/2005 of 04/12/2005 on tax procedures.

[142] Art. 1.2 of the law n° 74/2008 of 31/12/2008 modifying and complementing law n° 25/2005 of 04/12/2005 on tax procedures.

[143] Art. 1, 3, 4 of the law n° 74/2008 of 31/12/2008 modifying and complementing law n° 25/2005 of 04/12/2005 on tax procedures.

audit or issue oriented audit, the period of seven (7) days mentioned above is reduced to three (3) days.[144]

II.5.1.1.3. Entrance to premises without notice

An authorized officer may visit and enter into public premises of the taxpayer or of any other person between 7:00 am to 6:00 pm, without issuing any written notification. He or she may also request to enter private buildings that are assumed to be business related.

In case the authorized officer wants access to private buildings or premises and when no access was given, the Prosecution may give a search warrant to the Tax Administration. If the prosecution gives the search warrant, its copy shall be given to the taxpayer during the search. In case the tax administration has the permission to conduct search, it may seek the assistance of the governor of the province or City of Kigali, the commander of Police or the Mayor of the District or Town in order for the search to be conducted.

II.5.1.1.4. Estimated assessment procedure

Under Rwandan law, the Tax Administration is entitled to the right of starting estimated assessment procedure (*procedure d'imposition d'office*) when[145] (a) no tax declaration has been made; (b) a tax declaration was filed after the day mentioned in the law on taxes and there was no proof given of "force majeure" justifying the delay in filing; (c) the tax declaration was not signed by a competent person; (d) the tax declaration was not accompanied by all necessary documents; (e) the taxpayer was unwilling to cooperate with a tax audit officers or did

---

[144] Art. 20 *bis* of the law n° 25/2005 as modified by article 1 of the law n° 74/2008 of 31/12/2008 modifying and complementing law n° 25/2005 of 04/12/2005 on tax procedures.

[145] Art. 28 of the law n° 25/2005.

not provide the information requested; (f) books and records were not kept as provided by law; or (g) there are serious indications of tax fraud.

In the event of estimated assessment procedure, the Tax Administration sends a "note of an assessment procedure without notice" to the taxpayer. The note contains all reasons why the assessment procedure without notice was conducted. It may also contain fines in case of non-compliance with the tax law. All proofs available to the Tax Administration can be used to carry out an assessment procedure without notice.[146]

The taxpayer has the right to give written observations and remarks to the notice of an estimated assessment procedure within a period of thirty (30) days. He or she may also transmit additional evidence to the Tax Administration to prove that the estimated assessment procedure was not correctly conducted. The taxpayer has the right to a hearing if he or she requested for it in his or her reply.[147] The estimated assessment procedure may be applied in a period of five (5) years, starting from January 1st, following the tax period. Thus, a notice of estimated assessment has to be issued at least on the last day of the five (5) year period.[148]

II.5.1.1.5. Extending the deadline for filing tax returns

The taxpayer may apply to the Commissioner General of Rwanda Revenue Authority for an extension of the

---

[146] Art. 8 parag. 1 of the law nº 01/2012 of 03/02/2012 modifying and complementing law nº 25/2005 of 04/12/2005 on tax procedures as modified and complemented to date, in *O.G.* nº 13 of 26/03/2012.
[147] Art. 6.2 of the law n° 74/2008 of 31/12/2008 modifying and complementing law n° 25/2005 of 04/12/2005 on tax procedures.
[148] Art. 6.4 of the law n° 74/2008 of 31/12/2008 modifying and complementing law n° 25/2005 of 04/12/2005 on tax procedures.

deadline for filing the tax declaration if sufficient proof of the reasons and difficulties faced in filing the tax declaration on time is given.[149]
The taxpayer makes a written request to the Commissioner General before the original filing date expires. The Commissioner General may provide the taxpayer in writing with an extension of the deadline for filing the tax declaration. Extension of a deadline for tax declaration does not suspend the accrual of "interests for late payment". In addition, such extension will protect the tax payer against the "fine for late payment"[150] and the procedure of "estimated assessment" (*imposition d'office*).[151]

II.5.1.2. Paying the due tax

After tax declaration, another main duty of a taxpayer towards the Tax Administration is to pay the due tax.

II.5.1.2.1. Possibility of paying taxes in instalments

The taxpayer may apply to the Commissioner General of Rwanda Revenue Authority for paying in instalments. The Commissioner General has the competence to set out the rules and conditions to apply for such an instalment payment. Payment in instalments cannot exceed one year. Failure of the taxpayer to pay under the conditions of the instalment plan results in an immediate obligation to pay the remaining amount due.[152]

The request to pay in instalment is submitted to the Commissioner General upon fulfilment of some

---

[149] Art. 16 of the law n° 25/2005.
[150] Art. 61 al. 2 of the law n° 25/2005.
[151] Art. 28 of the law n° 25/2005.
[152] Art. 47 of the law n° 25/2005.

conditions[153] namely to (a) provide a proof of payment of an amount worth at least 25% of the tax due; (b) to have regularly paid taxes and duties correctly; (c) not to have been implicated in use of forged documents on taxes and duties; (e) to provide a guarantee acceptable to the Tax Administration. The Commissioner General, may allow a taxpayer to pay in instalments without necessarily executing a guarantee based on circumstantial evidence of hardship or a proved compliance record of the taxpayer.[154]

II.5.1.2.2. Waive of tax liability, interest and penalties

The taxpayer can apply in writing for a waiver of tax liability, interest on late payments and administrative fines in case of substantial hardships indicating no ability to clear the tax liability.[155] However, a waiver cannot be granted to persons proved having committed offences of understating or evading taxes.[156] The waiver is applied for in the note sent to the Commissioner General and if the tax administration finds that the request of the taxpayer is founded, it makes a report to the Minister of finance for a decision on penalties, interest of late payment or principle tax, and the same report is also transmitted to the Cabinet in order to make final decisions.[157]

---

[153] Art. 2.1 of the Commissioner General Rules n° 008/2009 of 07/12/2009 modifying and completing the Commissioner General Rules n° 002/2007 of 15/06/2007 implementing the law n° 25/2005 of 04/12/2005 on tax procedures.

[154] Art. 2.3 and 2.1 of the Commissioner General Rules n° 008/2009 of 07/12/2009 modifying and completing the Commissioner General Rules n° 002/2007 of 15/06/2007 implementing the law n° 25/2005 of 04/12/2005 on tax procedures.

[155] Art. 16 parag.1 of the law nº 01/2012 of 03/02/2012 modifying and complementing law nº 25/2005 of 04/12/2005 on tax procedures as modified and complemented to date, in *O.G.* nº 13 of 26/03/2012.

[156] *Ibidem.*

[157] *Idem,* art. 16 parag. 2.

II.5.1.2.3. Prescription

Under Rwandan law, when taxes were not paid within a period of ten (10) years counting from the time it was due, the Tax Administration loses the right to claim the tax to be paid (*Droit de rappel*).[158]

II.5.1.3. Other duties of taxpayer

Taxpayer has some other duties like a duty to register as taxpayer as well as some duties that are specific to VAT registered taxpayers.

II.5.1.3.1. Duty to register

Any person who sets up a business or other activities that may be taxable is obliged to register with the Tax Administration within a period of seven (7) days from the beginning of the business or activity or the establishment of the company.[159] The tax administration assigns a taxpayer identification number (TIN) to be used for all taxes.[160] In addition to a duty to register, other taxpayer's duties include the duty to keep books and other documents required by the law[161] the duty to give free access to books and other documents whenever it is required by an authorised fiscal officer[162] and comply with the duties specific to VAT in case the taxpayer is VAT registered.

II.5.1.3.2. Duty to register for VAT

Any person who carries out taxable activities exceeding twenty million Rwanda Francs (20,000,000 RWF) in the previous fiscal year, or five million Rwanda Francs (5,000,000 RWF) in the preceding calendar quarter is required to register for VAT with the tax administration

[158] Art. 46.2 of the law n° 25/2005.
[159] Art. 10.1 of the law n° 25/2005.
[160] Art. 11.1 of the law n° 25/2005.
[161] Art. 12, 13 and 15.1 of the law n° 25/2005.
[162] Art. 22 and 23 of the law n° 25/2005.

within a period of seven (7) days from the end of the year or from the end of the quarter mentioned above.[163]

II.5.1.3.3. Duty to use prescribed VAT invoice

A Value Added Tax invoice is an accounting document prepared in the form determined by the Tax Administration and which shows the following information:[164] names of the taxpayer and the client, and the taxpayer's trade name, if different from the personal name; taxpayer identification number and the purchaser's if necessary; number and date of the value added tax registration certificate; description of goods sold or services rendered; value of taxable goods or services; sum of Value Added Tax due on the given taxable transaction; date on which the Value Added Tax invoice was issued; and the serial number of the Value Added Tax invoice.

II.5.2. Fiscal litigation: Settlement of fiscal disputes

In fiscal matters, the procedure of settling disputes differs depending on whether the concerned tax is collected by the Government (centralized) or by the district (decentralized).

II.5.2.1. The procedure for centralised taxes

Two types of appeals are open to a taxpayer who wants to contest the tax levied onto him or the fiscal sanction imposed: Administrative appeal and judicial appeal.

II.5.2.1.1. Administrative appeal

The taxpayer who is not satisfied with the contents of the tax assessment notice may appeal to the Commissioner General within thirty (30) days after receipt of the

---

[163] Art. 10.2 of the law n° 25/2005.

[164] Art. 14 of the law n° 25/2005.

"assessment notice" (*note d'imposition*).[165] In principle, the appeal does not suspend the obligation to pay tax, interest and penalties. However, upon written request by the taxpayer, the Commissioner General may suspend payment of the disputed amount of tax for the duration of the appeal.[166] The Commissioner General makes a decision on the appeal within a period of thirty (30) days and sends it to the taxpayer.[167] The Commissioner General or any other competent staff of the Tax Administration designated by the Commissioner General may extend this period once for another thirty (30) days and informs the taxpayer and when no decision is taken by the Commissioner General within this period, the appeal is assumed to have a basis.[168]

II.5.2.1.2. Judicial appeal

The taxpayer who is not satisfied with the decision of the Commissioner General may make a judicial appeal. The appeal is brought before the competent tribunal within a period of thirty (30) days after the receipt of the Commissioner General's decision.[169]

II.5.2.2. The procedure for decentralised taxes

Again, there are two types of appeals with respect to taxes collected by the Districts: administrative appeal and judicial appeal.

---

[165] Art. 30 of the law n° 25/2005.

[166] Art. 31.2 of the law n° 25/2005.

[167] Art. 9 parag. 1 of the law n° 01/2012 of 03/02/2012 modifying and complementing law n° 25/2005 of 04/12/2005 on tax procedures as modified and complemented to date, in *O.G.* n° 13 of 26/03/2012.

[168] *Idem,* art. 9 parag. 2.

[169] Art. 38 of the law n° 25/2005 as amended by art. 7 of the law n° 74/2008 of 31/12/2008 modifying and complementing the law n° 25/2005 of 04/12/2005.

II.5.2.2.1. Administrative appeal

Any complaint regarding payment of taxes and their recovery are handled by the council of the District or Town where the taxable items are located.[170]

II.5.2.2.2. Judicial appeal

If the taxpayer is not satisfied with the decision taken by the Council, he/she refers the matter to the competent court. In that case, the confiscation of assets is suspended until the court gives its verdict.[171]

II.5.3. Evidences in tax law

Evidences in tax law can be assessed reference made to the burden of proof as well as the types of evidences, which are admitted in tax disputes.

II.5.3.1. The burden of proof

Fiscal declaration is the first source of information that revenue authority can base on to assume the burden of evidence. In fact, since the taxpayer produces a declaration showing his/her situation, it is up to the revenue authority to agree or disagree with already established declaration.

If revenue authority disagrees with it, it is up to revenue authority to prove that the declaration is wrong, by showing the existence and the extent of the alleged non declared tax. Thus, the revenue authority must not only prove that a given tax base has not been declared but also to prove the link between the taxpayer and tax base as well as in which category of taxes it falls in.

---

[170] Art. 33.2 of the law n° 17/2002 of 10/05/2002 establishing the source of revenue for districts and towns and its management.
[171] Art. 33.4 of the law n° 17/2002 of 10/05/2002.

The rule is simple to understand. It is the revenue authority that seeks the payment of tax. So, it is up to it to prove that the conditions required by the law are fulfilled. To this rule, there is only one exception, that's in case a taxpayer is claiming a deduction. In such cases, it is the taxpayer who has the burden to prove that he/she has right to that deduction and precise how much must be deducted. The same is when he/she applies for exoneration or for correcting an involuntary error.[172]

Grossomodo, it is an application of the general principle of law *Actori Incumbit Probatio*, according to which it is generally accepted in legal matter that the burden of proof falls to the head of the person who is claiming a given right. This principle is however completed by another important one, that's *Reus Fit Excipiendo*, i.e. the burden of proof falls to the head of the person who is claiming having executed an obligation that he/she was previously charged with.[173]

Though, the burden of proof lies with Tax Administration when[174] rectifying tax declaration of the taxpayer; indicating the method of proof based on signs and indications of prosperity; it applies for permission from prosecutor to ask questions from a person bound by professional secrecy as described in paragraph 4 of article 4 of the law on tax procedure; applying to the Prosecutor for search warrant as described in paragraph 2 of article 25 of the law on tax procedure.

---

[172] Art. 45 of the law on tax procedures.

[173] More details on these principles can be found in A. M. Ngagi, *Cours de droit civil des obligations*, Manuel pour étudiants, Butare, Les éditions de l'Université Nationale du Rwanda, 2004, p. 258.

[174] Art. 44 of the law on tax procedures.

Similarly, the burden of proof lies with the taxpayer when[175] the tax administration conducts a tax assessment without notice; the taxpayer starts an appeal procedure to correct an unintentional error in tax declaration; and the taxpayer wants to disprove the content of an affidavit.

II.5.3.2. Types of evidences

The Rwandan tax law recognises two set of evidences namely ordinary evidences and special evidences.

II.5.3.2.1. Ordinary evidences

All ordinary types of proofs are allowed to the tax administration except the oath.[176] However, the minister, through a Ministerial Order, determines the types and the use of electronic evidence.[177] This means that accepted evidences are written evidences, witnesses, presumptions and confession/admission of the taxpayer. With regard to the nature of tax disputes, the most useful evidences are written and presumptions.

II.5.3.2.2. Signs and indications of prosperity

When the Tax Administration establishes that a taxpayer shows signs and indications of prosperity in a certain fiscal year, and the taxpayer cannot give an explanation for this apparent prosperity, the Tax Administration may add the value of these signs and indications to the taxable income of the taxpayer and use this as a method of proof.[178] When using this method of proof, the Tax Administration gives to the taxpayer all proof it uses to indicate the signs and indications of prosperity, as well as the methods of valuation of the cost or value.[179]

---

[175] Art. 45 of the law on tax procedures.
[176] Art. 42 parag. 1 of the law on tax procedures.
[177] Art. 42 parag. 2 of the law on tax procedures.
[178] Art. 43 parag. 1 of the law on tax procedures.
[179] Art. 43 parag. 2 of the law on tax procedures.

This is a presumption *iuris tantum*, where the Tax Administration presumes that if there are signs of enrichment of a given taxpayer, that such enrichment comes from non declared revenues. In other words, here the Tax Administration considers that all expenditures that the taxpayer cannot explain the source are a result of non declared revenues. Signs and indications of prosperity as evidence cannot base itself on simple presumptions because it is a general rule that a presumption cannot simply base on presumption.

II.5.3.2.3. Affidavits

Under Rwandan law, Affidavits are provided for by article 40 and 41 of the law on tax procedures. In terms of article 40 of the law on tax procedures, an authorized officer, responsible for carrying out audits and investigations, has the power to make affidavits. An affidavit is drawn up in the exercise of the authorized officer's duties. It contains facts and evidence the authorized officer has personally established. It has to indicate clearly the name of the authorized officer, the name, address and activity of the taxpayer and the date on which it has been made. It is jointly signed by the authorized officer and the suspect and a copy of the affidavit has to be sent to the taxpayer.

As far as the legal character of the affidavit[180] is concerned, an affidavit constitutes sufficient proof of the facts and evidence the authorized officer has established. It may be used by the Tax Administration for issuing an assessment without notice and it may be used as testimony. The contents of the affidavit can only be disregarded if it is proved that the authorized officer committed fraud or made a serious mistake.

---

[180] Art. 41 of the law on tax procedures.

II.5.4. Fiscal sanctions

We distinguish between sanctions relating to taxes collected by the Government and sanctions relating to taxes collected by the districts.

II.5.4.1. Sanctions applicable to centralised taxes

Here we distinguish between sanctions imposed by the Tax Administration and those imposed by the courts.

II.5.4.1.1. Sanctions imposed by tax administration

Under Rwandan law, different sanctions are imposed by the tax administration. Such sanctions imposed by the tax administration are:

a) Interests for late payment[181]

In the event the taxpayer fails to pay tax within the period set forth by the Law, he or she is required to pay interest on the amount of tax. The interest rate is fixed at 1.5%. Interest is calculated on a monthly basis, non-compounding, counting from the first day after the tax should have been paid until the day of payment, which is included. Every month started is considered as a complete month.

Interest shall always be payable, even when the taxpayer has lodged an administrative appeal or a judicial appeal against the assessment. Interest accrues cannot exceed one hundred percent (100%) of the amount of tax. When the taxpayer pays, the payment shall be used in paying taxes by deducting interest, penalties and tax liability.

---

[181] Art. 12 of the law n° 01/2012 of 03/02/2012 modifying and complementing law n° 25/2005 of 04/12/2005 on tax procedures as modified and complemented to date, in *O.G.* n° 13 of 26/03/2012.

b) Fines

Under Rwandan law, different fines are possible like fixed fines, fines for late payment, fines for understatement of taxes, fines for VAT violations, fines for tax fraud and fines for failure to pay withheld taxes.

i) Fixed fines[182]

A taxpayer or any person is subject to a fixed fine if he/she fails to file a tax declaration on time; to file a withholding declaration on time; to withhold tax; to provide proofs required by the Tax Administration; to cooperate with a tax audit; to communicate on time the capacity or appointment he or she has been given as described by the paragraph 2 of Article 7 of Law n° 25/2005 of 04/12/2005 on tax procedures; to register as described by article 10 of Law n° 25/2005 of 04/12/2005 on tax procedures; to comply with articles 12 and 13 (keeping required books) and 15 (books required for a company) and 14 (use the prescribed VAT invoice) of Law n° 25/2005 of 04/12/2005 on tax procedures; to pay on time the profit tax advance. A non-compliance with above obligations results into fines.

Fines related to violations of above mentioned obligations are set as follow:

- one hundred thousand (100,000) Rwanda francs if the taxpayer's annual turnover is equal to or less than twenty million (20,000,000) RWF;
- three hundred thousand (300,000) Rwanda francs if the taxpayer's annual turnover exceeds twenty million (20,000,000) Rwanda francs;
- five hundred thousand (500,000) Rwanda francs if the taxpayer was informed by the Tax

[182] Art. 9 of the law n°74/2008 of 31/12/2008 modifying and complementing law n° 25/2005 of 04/12/2005 on tax procedures.

Administration that he or she is in a large taxpayer[183] category.

In case the same violation is committed twice within five (5) years, the fine is twice the original fine. In case the same violation is committed again within such five (5) years, the fine is four times the original fine.

ii) Fines for late payment[184]

If the amount of tax shown on a tax declaration or the amount of tax which is the result of an adjusted assessment by the Tax Administration is not paid in time, the taxpayer is subject to a fine of ten percent (10%) of the tax payable. The taxpayer is not subject to this fine if the Commissioner General provided an extension for filing the tax declaration according to article sixteen (16) of the Law n° 25/2005. The late payment fine does not apply to interest or administrative fine.

iii) Fines for understatement of tax[185]

If the amount of tax shown on a tax declaration understates the amount of tax required to be shown as a consequence of an audit or investigation by the Tax Administration, the taxpayer is subject to the following fine:

- five per cent (5%) of the amount of the understatement if the understatement is equal to or more than five per cent (5%) but less than ten percent (10 %) of the tax liability;

---

183 Under Rwandan law, "Large Taxpayer" means any taxpayer who has been notified by Rwanda Revenue Authority that he/she is registered among large taxpayers following the directives of the Commissioner General (Art. 2 of the law n° 25/2005).

184 Art. 61 of the law n° 25/2005.

185 Art. 10 of the law n° 74/2008 of 31/12/2008 modifying and complementing law n° 25/2005 of 04/12/2005 on tax procedures.

- ten per cent (10%) of the amount of the understatement if the understatement is equal to or more than ten percent (10%) but less than twenty percent (20 %) of the tax liability he or she ought to have paid;
- twenty per cent (20%) of the amount of the understatement if the understatement is twenty percent (20%) or more but less than fifty percent (50%) of the tax liability he or she ought to have paid;
- fifty per cent (50%) of the amount of the understatement if the understatement is fifty percent (50%) or more of the tax liability he or she ought to have paid.

The taxpayer, who rectifies his or her tax declaration before he or she is notified of imminent control of his or her declaration, shall not be subject to the fine mentioned above.

iv) Fines for Value Added Tax violations[186]

The following administrative fines are imposed to persons who do not comply with provisions of Value Added Tax law:

- in the event of operation without VAT registration where VAT registration is required, fifty per cent (50%) of the amount of VAT payable for the entire period of operation without VAT registration;
- in the event of the incorrect issuance of a VAT invoice resulting in a decrease in the amount of VAT payable or in an increase of the VAT input credit or in the event of the failure to issue a VAT invoice, one hundred per cent (100%) of the

[186] Art. 11 of the law n° 74/2008 of 31/12/2008.

amount of VAT for the invoice or on the transaction;

- for issuing of a VAT invoice by a person who is not registered for VAT is assessed a penalty of one hundred per cent (100%) of the VAT which is indicated in that VAT invoice and is due to pay the VAT as indicated on that VAT invoice.

v) Fine for tax fraud[187]

Taxpayer who commits fraud is subject to an administrative fine of one hundred percent (100%) of the evaded tax. In addition to that penalty, the Tax Administration refers the case to the Prosecution service if the taxpayer voluntarily evaded such tax, like use of false accounts, falsified documents or any other act punishable by Law. In case of conviction, the taxpayer can be imprisoned for a period between six (6) months and two (2) years. The Minister's order determines an award given to any person who denounces a taxpayer who engages in tax fraud.

vi) Fines for failure to pay tax withheld[188]

In case a person intentionally fails to deliver the tax withheld to the Tax Administration, he or she is subject to a fine of one hundred per cent (100%) of the unpaid tax. In addition, the Tax Administration refers the case to the Prosecution service. In case of conviction, the taxpayer can be imprisoned for a period between three (3) months and two (2) years.

---

[187] Art. 12 of the law n° 74/2008 of 31/12/2008.
[188] Art. 13 of the law n° 74/2008 of 31/12/2008.

c) Additional Penalties[189]

Additional penalties include the closure of business activities for a period of thirty (30) days and publication in nationwide newspapers.

II.5.4.1.2. Sanctions imposed by the courts

Sanctions imposed by the courts are imprisonment and some other additional penalties if need be. Imprisonment occurs in case of tax fraud[190] as well as in case of failure to pay withheld tax.[191] Additional penalties that may be imposed by the courts are being banned from bidding for public tenders and withdrawal of a business register (also called "trade licence").[192]

II.5.4.2. Sanctions applicable to decentralised taxes

Sanctions applicable to taxes collected by the district are the surcharges and interests for late payment.

---

189 Art. 67 of the law no 25/2005.

190 Art. 64 of the law nº 25/2005.

191 Art. 65 of the law nº 25/2005.

192 Art. 67 of the law nº 25/2005.

a) Surcharges

Where declaration has either not been made, is made late, is fraudulent or incomplete, the taxpayer pays a surcharge equal to 40% of the amount due.[193]

b) Interest for late payment

Taxes not paid in the specified time bear such interest for the District or Town as is determined by the District or Town Council. However, this interest cannot exceed 1.25% per each month of late payment, and must be calculated from the date the taxes were due to the date they are paid.[194]

II.5.5. Forced recovery

When a tax is not paid voluntarily within the prescribed time, the Tax Administration proceeds to forced recovery. A distinction is also made between taxes collected by the Government and taxes collected by the Districts.

II.5.5.1. The procedure for centralised taxes

The forced recovery for taxes collected by the Government starts with a warning followed by a seizure and auction of property of the defaulting taxpayer.

II.5.5.1.1. Warning

If a tax is not paid within seven (7) days from the receipt of a "notice of assessment", the Tax Administration sends a warning letter to the taxpayer, indicating the amount of tax, interest and penalties to be paid and the legal action that will follow if the tax, interest and penalties are not paid within fifteen (15) days from the delivery of the

---

193 Art. 9 of the law n° 33/2003 of 06/9/2003 modifying and complementing law n°17/2002 of 10/05/2002 establishing the source of revenue for districts and towns and its management.

194 *Idem,* art. 10.

warning letter.[195] The fifteen (15) day period may be disregarded in case the possibilities for effective tax collection are in jeopardy.[196]

II.5.5.1.2. Seizure and auction of taxpayer's property

When tax is not paid within fifteen (15) days from the delivery of the warning letter, the Tax Administration may seize any movable or immovable property of the taxpayer, whether held by the taxpayer or any other person.[197] The seized property is sold under a public auction after eight (8) days the taxpayer is notified of the affidavit (*procès-verbal de saisie*).[198]

II.5.5.1.3. Notification to third parties

If a tax is not paid within fifteen (15) days as mentioned in article 46, the Tax Administration may require any debtors, bankers and other persons in possession of a taxpayer's funds to pay to the Tax Administration the amount due to the taxpayer against the taxpayer's tax liability.[199]

The debtor has the obligation within a period of fifteen (15) days from the time of receipt of the note from the tax administration to[200] give written explanations to the Tax Administration of the amount due or notify the Tax Administration in writing that he or she owed no debt to the taxpayer by the time when the Tax Administration notified him or her and pay the debt which is equivalent to

---

[195] Art. 46.1 and 18.2 of the law n° 25/2005.
[196] Art. 46.2 of the law n° 25/2005.
[197] Art. 48.1 of the law n° 25/2005.
[198] Art. 48.1 of the law n° 25/2005.
[199] Art. 49.1 of the law n° 25/2005 as modified by article 8 of the law n°74/2008 of 31/12/2008 modifying and complementing law n° 25/2005 of 04/12/2005 on tax procedures.
[200] Art. 49.3 of the law n° 25/2005.

the tax in accordance with the contract with the taxpayer or with respect to obligations to the taxpayer.

If the debtor does not comply with the conditions mentioned above, he or she is assumed as liable to debt of the Tax Administration the amount equal to tax liability.[201] If the debtor complies with these conditions, he or she is discharged of the debt liability to the taxpayer for the amount paid to the Tax Administration.[202]

II.5.5.2. The procedure for descentralised taxes

The procedure for forced recovery for taxes collected by the districts starts with warning before proceeding to seizure and auction procedures.

II.5.5.2.1. Warning

In case a taxpayer is tracked that he/she has not paid the tax in the stipulated time, the District or Town tax collector sends to the taxpayer, after approval by the Executive Committee, a warning letter reminding him/her to pay within 15 days.[203]

II.5.5.2.2. Seizure and auction of taxpayer's property

Where the period of 15 days provided for by Article 34 of Law n° 17/2002 of 10/05/2002 expires, the tax collector shall wait for eight (8) days before confiscation. After thirty (30) days from reception of the minutes of seizure of his or her goods by the tax payer, the goods seized shall be auctioned.[204]

---

[201] Art. 49.4 of the law nº 25/2005.

[202] Art. 49.5 of the law nº 25/2005.

[203] Art. 34 of the law nº 17/2002 of 10/05/2002.

[204] Art. 12 of the law nº 33/2003 of 06/9/2003 modifying and complementing law n°17/2002 of 10/05/2002 establishing the source of revenue for districts and towns and its management

II.5.5.2.3. Notification to third parties

The District or Town tax collector may also ask any debtors, bankers, etc of the defaulting taxpayer to pay to the Tax Administration the amount due to the taxpayer against the taxpayer's tax liability.[205] In case of non payment of taxes by the notified third party within eight (8) days as from the date the order to pay was received, they shall be held liable for those tax debts in place of the taxpayer.[206]

II.6. International aspects of Rwanda tax system

International taxation has got many aspects and this part is only limited to issues relating to permanent establishment, e-commerce taxation and implications of regional integration on Rwandan taxation.

II.6.1. Permanent establishment under Rwandan law

Fair taxation of an internationally-organized business requires an equitable allocation between the various jurisdictions of the tax base of the business. Even though, there are no clear criteria for the international allocation of costs and profits between home and host countries,[207] which leads to the concept of permanent establishment. According to article 5 of the OECD Model Tax Convention, permanent establishment means a fixed place of business through which the business of an enterprise is wholly or partly carried on. In article 5 of the law n° 16/2005 of 18/08/2005 on direct taxes on income, the Rwandan legislator has adopted *mutatis mutandis* the same definition as the OECD.[208]

---

205 Art. 11.3 of the law n° 33/2003 of 06/9/2003.

206 Art. 11.5 of the law n° 33/2003 of 06/9/2003.

207 S. Piciotto, *International Business Taxation*, London, Claphan High Street, 1992, p. 4.

208 Art. 5 of the law n° 16/2005 of 18/08/2005 on direct taxes on income compared to art. 5 of the OECD Model Tax Convention.

II.6.2. Taxation of electronic commerce in Rwanda

In Rwanda, electronic commerce (e-commerce) is governed by the law n° 18/2010 of 12/05/2010 relating to electronic messages, electronic signatures and electronic transactions.[209] Unfortunately, this law doesn't define what e-commerce is. According to D. S. Evans, D. D. Garcia-Swart and B. G. Martin-Keating[210], e-commerce refers to business that is conducted online, usually over the internet.[211] Within the World Trade Organisation, the term e-commerce is used as the production, distribution, marketing, sale, or delivery of goods and services by electronic means.[212] E-commerce is also defined as a set of commercial activities concluded via electronic network, like internet, including online promotion and sales of goods and services as well as exchange of correspondence.[213]

Generally considered, the taxation of e-commerce raises a number of some legal issues, like to know where a business is to be regarded as established for tax purposes? on which territory do cyberspace transactions take place? where and when taxes can be collected? which legal system will apply? to what extent is it possible to apply

---

[209] In Official Gazette n° 20 of 17/05/2010.

[210] D. S. Evans, D. D. Garcia-Swart & B. G. Martin-Keating, "The Failure of E-Commerce Businesses: A Surprise or Not?", *European Business Organization Law Review*, 2002, p. 3.

[211] However, the terminology in the literature and popular press is not always consistently defined. The U.S.Census Bureau uses the following definitions: e-business processes (how business is conducted), e-commerce transactions (buying and selling) and e-infrastructure (which support electronic activities). For more details, cfr *Ibid.*

[212] V. Sacha Wunsch, "The Internet, Cross-border Trade in Services, and the GATS: Lessons from US-Gambling", *World Trade Review*, 2006, p. 319.

[213] *Ibid.*

rules of international law? Existence of harmonized laws or legal instruments, at international level, regarding e-commerce taxation? Reformation of tax laws to better cope with e-commerce developments? Etc.

The same challenges do exist in Rwanda, and although the Rwandan legislator has managed to set up a law on e-commerce, there is still a gap on appropriate and specific law on taxation of e-commerce. Again, the practice on e-commerce taxation is still low. However, this is not a problem of only Rwanda as the phenomenon of e-commerce puts a strain on traditional concepts of international tax law.

II.6.3. EAC regional integration and impact on taxes

The accelerating process of globalization of trade and investment has fundamentally changed the relationship among domestic tax systems. According to OECD, the process of globalization has led to increased competition among businesses in the global market place.[214] By the same vein, globalization has had many positive effects on the development of tax systems; however, it has also had the negative effects of opening up new ways by which companies and individuals can minimize and avoid taxes and in which countries can exploit these new opportunities by developing tax policies aimed primarily at diverting financial and other geographically mobile capital.[215]

Regional integration constitutes one of the processes that enhances the harmonization and coordination of tax laws among member states. Rwanda is member to different regional organizations but so far East African Community

[214] OECD Report: Harmful Tax Competition, An Emerging Global Issue. 1998.
[215] *Ibid.*

(EAC) is more active compared to other regional organizations that Rwanda is member.

Rwanda joined East African Community in 2007. Although Rwanda's accession to the EAC is expected to bring considerable economic benefits in the medium to long term, membership imposes some fiscal constraints and Rwanda is already experiencing a reduction in customs revenue.[216]

Article 32(e) of the EAC Treaty requires that member states harmonise their tax policies and reform them to remove distortions and promote investment. The Customs Union, a common tariff for trade with the rest of world and a Common Market were introduced in 2010. A Monetary Union and a political federation are planned. At present the member states have huge differences in their tax systems and these differences sometimes result in unfair tax competition and unequal treatment of taxpayers, goods and services which if not addressed will distort the functioning of the Common Market.

Harmonisation of tax policies and laws on domestic taxation is therefore an essential aspect of microeconomic convergence and is one of the benchmarks to be attained for the effective functioning of the Common Market. The member states of the East African Community have committed themselves to eliminate harmful tax competition. Article 83(2)(e) of the *Treaty for the Establishment of the East African* Community commits the member states to harmonise tax policies with a view to remove tax distortions in order to bring about a more efficient allocation of resources.

---

[216] RRA Report, 2011.

The Protocol on the Establishment of the EAC Customs Union provides for the establishment of export promotion schemes, special economic zones and exemption regimes. However, at present the incentive and exemption fiscal regimes differ between the member states both in terms of the provisions in place and the generosity of the schemes.[217]

Additionally, the Draft Code of Conduct Against Harmful Tax Competition in the East African Community defines harmful tax competition as including: *the competition created within an economic block as a result of preferential tax regimes that offer tax advantages to particular entities at the detriment of other entities operating in the same country or other countries thereby putting other entities at a disadvantage* (p. 6). It further defines harmful tax practices as meaning: *Tax measures by tax havens and /or preferential tax regimes that affect the location of financial and other service activities, erode the tax base of other countries, distort trade and investment patterns and undermine the fairness, neutrality and the broad social acceptance of systems* (p. 6).

This Draft Code of Conduct against Harmful Tax Competition in the East African Community explicitly requires that in order to eliminate potentially harmful practices:

- any provisions for the negotiation of the tax rate or the tax base be reviewed;
- any tax laws which exempt foreign-source income from residency country taxation be reviewed;

[217] Mukibi 2010; Mbyamkono 2010.

- with respect to VAT, that an EAC common VAT model be developed and that zero-rated regimes and exempt transactions harmonised;
- With respect to income tax that initial capital allowances of more than 50 per cent are abolished, that all tax incentive regimes in the corporate income tax system, especially export processing zones and special economic zones, are reviewed and harmonised, that the treatment of losses and withholding taxes on dividends, interest payments, royalties and services are also harmonised and that capital gains from capital sales be treated as normal profit;
- With respect to excise duty that a harmonised legal base be developed which defines the categories of taxable goods, defines taxable items in a uniform way, replaces *ad valorem* rates with specific rates and defines the lower and upper ceilings for national tax rates. Tax rates should be defined in the national excise duty laws and discriminatory rates for imported goods should be abolished.

The *Code* provides for special consideration to be given to tax measures that are designed to support the economic development of a particular region, including paying special attention to the particular features and constraints of the partner states that are geographically disadvantaged. Rwanda along with Burundi both suffer from being small countries, landlocked and with a long distance to ports. They are also disadvantaged by the high non-tariff costs of exporting and importing goods.[218] It should, however, be noted that in marketing the proposed Kigali Free Trade Zone the government of Rwanda emphasises the access to

[218] Ministry of Trade and Industry and Private Sector Federation 2010.

a large market accessible from the location that is not easily served by other trade routes in the region.[219]

---

[219] IPAR, East African Taxation Project: Rwanda Country Case Study, June 2011, pp. 12-13.

Postface

IMIKORANIRE Y'U RWANDA N'IBINDI BIHUGU BIGIZE UMURYANGO WA AFURIKA Y'IBURASIRAZUBA MU BIJYANYE N'IMISORO

By TWAHIRWA Jean Baptiste*

Umuryango wa Afurika y'iburasirazuba ugizwe n'ibihugu bitanu (5) aribyo Kenya, Tanzaniya, Uganda, Uburundi n'u Rwanda.[220] U Rwanda rwinjiye mu muryango w'ibihugu bya Afurika y'iburasizuba muri Nyakanga 2007.[221] Zimwe mu ntego z'uyu muryango, ni uguhuza za gasutamo ku bihugu bigize umuryango[222] no guhuza mu bijyanye n'ibipimo by'amahoro yakwa ku bicuruzwa bikomoka hanze y'umuryango.[223] Guhuza ku bijyanye n'imisoreshereze y'ibihugu bigize uyu muryango kandi, bigamije gufata kimwe abacuruzi n'abasoreshwa bakomoka muri ibyo bihugu, bityo kugira ngo intego zo gukuraho inzitizi z'ubucuruzi zishingiye ku misoreshereze[224], iterambere ry'ubucuruzi n'ubukungu muri rusange[225], n'ishyirwaho ry'isoko rusange hagati

---

* Holds a LLM in Business Law and he is a State Attorney at Rwanda Revenue Authority and visiting lecturer of Business Law at Adventist University of Central Africa.

220 East African Community, "*EAC Customs Valuation Manual: A guide to the Customs of Valuation of Imported Goods in the East African Community*", Arusha, 2012.

221 E. Kafeero, "*Customs and trade facilitation in the East African Community (EAC)*", World Customs Journal, p. 63; available at www.ssrn.com, accessed on 5 November 2014.

222 Ijambo "Umuryango" risobanura Umuryango w'Afurika y'Iburasirazuba.

223 Ingingo ya 75 y'Amasezerano ashyiraho umuryango w'ibihugu by'Afurika y'Iburasirazuba yo muri 1999. Ijambo "*Umuryango*" risobanura umuryango wa Afurika y'Iburasirazuba.

224 Ingingo ya 75, 1(b) y'Amasezerano ashyiraho umuryango.

225 S. Khorana, K. Kimbugwe & N. Perdikis, "The *impact of tarrif reductions under the East African Community Customs Union: Intra-*

y'ibihugu bigize uyu muryango zibashe kugerwaho.[226] Muri urwo rwego, mu mwaka wa 2004 hashyizweho Itegeko rigenga za Gasutamo z'Umuryango w'Afurika y'Iburasirazuba[227] n'Inyandikofatizo (*protocol*) yerekeye ishyirwaho ry'ubumwe bwa za gasutamo.[228] Ku bijyanye n'imisoro yakwa imbere mu bihugu bigize umuryango, mu mwaka wa 2010 hasinywe amasezerano yo kudasoresha inshuro ebyiri umusoro ku musaruro hagati y'ibihugu bigize umuryango[229]; u Rwanda rukaba rwarayashyizeho umukono. U Rwanda kandi rwagiye rusinya amasezerano y'ubufatanye atandukanye n'ibihugu bigize umuryango; ndetse rugatangiza imishinga itandukanye, mu rwego rwo gushyira mu bikorwa amategeko agenga umuryango.

I. Imikorere ya za gasutamo zo muri EAC'ibihugu bigize umuryango

Kimwe n'ibindi bihugu bigize umuryango w'Afurika y'Iburasirazuba, ku bijyanye n'amahoro yishyuzwa ku bicuruzwa byinjira n'ibisohoka mu gihugu, u Rwanda rukurikiza amategeko agenga za gasutamo z'ibihugu bigize uwo muryango. Muri rusange, imikorere ya za Gasutamo igengwa n'itegeko rigenga za Gasutamo z'Umuryango w'Afurika y'Iburasirazuba ryo mu mwaka wa 2004, Inyandikofatizo (*protocol*) yerekeye ishyirwaho

---

trade effects on Uganda", Research Peper , Ecomod, 2007, at www.ssrn.com, accessed on 5 November 2014; M. Ncube, Z. Brixiova & Q. Meng, "Can intra-regional trade act as a global shock absorber in Africa?", African Development Bank Group Working Paper Series, n°198, 2014, p. 7.

226 Art. 76 y'Amasezerano ashyiraho umuryango.

227 Reba Itegeko rigenga za Gasutamo z'umuryango wa Afurika y'iburasirazuba ryo muri 2004.

228 (*Protocol on the Establishment of the East African Community Customs Union, 2004 and any annexes thereto*)

229 Reba Agreement between the Republics of Rwanda, Burundi, Kenya, Uganda and the United Republic of Tanzania for the avoidance of double taxation and the prevention of fiscal evasion with respect to taxes on income of 30th November 2010.

ry'Ubumwe bwa za Gasutamo yo muri 2004, amabwiriza ashyirwaho n'inama y'Abaminisitiri, ndetse n'amahame yo mu mategeko mpuzamahanga akenerwa. Ayo mategeko ateganya imiyoborere n'ubuyobozi bwa za Gasutamo, inshingano zo kwishyura amahoro ya gasutamo ku bicuruzwa binyuzwa kuri za gasutamo ndetse n'ingamba ziteganywa n'itegeko mu kurwanya magendu[230] hagati y'ibihugu bigize umuryango.

I.1. Imiyoborere ya za gasutamo

Ku bijyanye n'imiyoborere ya gasutamo, turibanda ku bijyanye n'ubuyobozi bwa gasutamo, imikorere y'abakozi ba gasutamo, ndetse n'amasaha y'akazi ku bakozi ba gasutamo. Turavuga kandi ku kirangantego n'ibendera bya za gasutamo.

I.1.1. Ubuyobozi bwa gasutamo

Hashingiwe ku biteganywa n'itegeko rigenga za gasutamo, ubuyobozi bwa gasutamo, bushyirwaho n'inama y'abaminisitiri hakurikijwe amasezerano ashyiraho umuryango[231]. Ubu buyobozi bufite inshingano zo gushyiraho ingamba zo gukemura ibibazo byerekeye gasutamo n'ubucuruzi mu muryango no guhuza ibyo bikorwa mu bihugu bigize umuryango.[232] Ubuyobozi kandi bufatanije n'abashinzwe gucunga no kuyobora za gasutamo, bufite inshingano zo guhuza no gukurikirira hafi:

[230] "Magendu" ni ugutumiza, kwohereza, kunyuza, kwimurira cyangwa gutwara imbere cyangwa hanze y'ibihugu bigize umuryango, ibicuruzwa ugambiriye kunyereza amahoro, cyangwa guhunga amabwiriza aca, akumira cyangwa abuza gutumiza, kwohereza hanze, kunyuza mu gihugu, kwimurira cyangwa gutwara ibicuruzwa nk'ibyo. Reba Itegeko rigenga za Gasutamo, umutwe wa I, 2.

[231] Itegeko rigenga za gasutamo, Umutwe wa II, 3.

[232] Itegeko rigenga za gasutamo, Umutwe wa II, 3.

a. imicungire y'igitabo cy'ibipimo by'amahoro yakwa ku bicuruzwa bikomoka hanze y'umuryango ;
b. gushyira mu bikorwa amategeko agenga umuryango ;
c. kworohereza ubucuruzi nkuko biteganijwe mu ngingo ya 6 y'Inyandikofatizo ;
d. imicungire y'amategeko agenga inkomoko y'ibicuruzwa mu muryango ;
e. gukusanya no gutangaza imibare yerekeye ubucuruzi ;
f. gushyira mu bikorwa no guhuza ikoranabuhanga mu buyobozi bwa za gasutamo ;
g. amahugurwa mu bya za gasutamo ;
h. kugenzura imikorere myiza no gushishikariza abantu kwibwiriza gusora;
i. kwitabira ibiganiro ku bibazo bireba za gasutamo ;
j. n'uburyo ba Komiseri bashyira mu bikorwa itegeko rigenga za gasutamo.[233]

Ubuyobozi kandi mu nshingano buhabwa n'iri tegeko rigenga za gasutamo, bugomba kubahiriza amategeko buhabwa n'inama y'abaminisitiri no gukora indi mirimo bushobora guhabwa n'inama y'abaminisitiri; ndetse no kujya inama, byaba ngomba, bugaha umwe mu ba komiseri imwe mu mirimo bushinzwe gukora.[234] Ku bijyanye n'intego z'amategeko agenga za gasutamo, inama y'abaminisitiri igomba gutegura amabwiriza yerekeye gahunda y'akazi hagati y'ubuyobozi na za gasutamo; guteganya komite ishinzwe gufasha ubuyobozi, gutegura politike na gahunda ku micungire no ku buyobozi bwa za gasutamo; guhana amakuru hagati

233 Itegeko rigenga za Gasutamo, umutwe wa II, 4. "*Itegeko rigenga za gasutamo*" ni itegeko rigenga za gasutamo z'umuryango w'afurika y'iburasirazuba ryo muri 2004.
234. Itegeko rigenga za Gasutamo, umutwe wa II, 4(b),(3).

y'ubuyobozi na ba komiseri; n'ibindi bibazo byerekeye gahunda y'akazi hagati y'ubuyobozi na za gasutamo.[235]

Itegeko kandi riteganya ko hagomba gushyirwaho umukomiseri ushinzwe gucunga za gasutamo muri buri gihugu kigize umuryango, hubahirijwe amategeko y'ibihugu biwugize hamwe n'undi mukozi wa gasutamo ukenewe mu gucunga iryo tegeko n'imikorere myiza ya za gasutamo. Komiseri akaba ashinzwe gucunga no kugenzura gasutamo, kwakira no kubarura amahoro ya gasutamo muri buri gihugu kigize umuryango; itegeko kandi rikaba rimuha ububasha bwo guha buri mukozi wa gasutamo, uruhushya rwo gukoresha ububasha ahabwa n'iri tegeko, yifashishije ububasha afite.[236]

Umukozi wahawe akazi mu biro cyangwa umwanya uhoraho muri gasutamo, agomba kurahira no gushyira umukono ku rupapuro rw'indahiro ye, rwateganijwe ku mugereka wa mbere w'Itegeko ryavuzwe haruguru, ari imbere y'umucamanza cyangwa imbere ya Komiseri.[237]

I.1.2. Ikirangantego n'ibendera bya za gasutamo zunze ubumwe

Itegeko rigenga za gasutamo riteganya ko hagomba gushyirwaho ikirangantego cya za gasutamo zunze ubumwe gifite igishushanyo n'ibisobanuro byemejwe n'amabwiriza; ikirangantego cya za gasutamo zunze ubumwe kizakoreshwa nka kashe izwi hose ya za gasutamo, ndetse n'ibendera rya za gasutamo zunze ubumwe rifite igishushanyo n'ibisobanuro byemejwe n'amabwiriza.[238]

Ibendera rya za gasutamo zunze ubumwe n'ibendera ry'umuryango rikaba rigomba ryifashishwa mu

---

235 Itegeko rigenga za Gasutamo, umutwe wa II, 4(c).
236 Itegeko rigenga za Gasutamo, umutwe wa II, 5.
237 Itegeko rigenga za Gasutamo, umutwe wa II, 5(4).
238 Itegeko rigenga za Gasutamo, umutwe wa II, 6(1)

gutandukanya amato akoreshwa na za gasutamo n'andi asanzwe.[239]

I.1.3 Umukozi wa gasutamo ufite ububasha bw'umugenzacyaha wa polisi

Kugira ngo bashobore kubahiriza amategeko agenga gasutamo, itegeko riteganya ko buri mukozi wa gasutamo uri mu kazi ke, agomba kuba afite ububasha bwose, uburenganzira, uburenganzira bwihariye no kurindwa nk'umugenzacyaha wa polisi wa kimwe mu bihugu akoreramo.[240]

I.1.4. Amasaha y'akazi n'ahantu ho gukorera

Itegeko riha uburenganzira komiseri bwo gushyiraho iminsi n'amasaha y'akazi asanzwe ku bakozi ba gasutamo.[241] Ibyo aribyo byose, umukozi wa gasutamo ashobora gukora mu gihe kitari icy'amasaha y'akazi. Muri icyo gihe, umuntu ushaka gukorerwa imirimo n'umukozi wa gasutamo hanze y'ikigo no mu masaha atari ay'akazi, agomba kubisabira uruhushya ku mukozi ubifitiye ububasha, haba mu cyambu cyangwa ahandi hantu yifuza ko bakorera imirimo akeneye, hakoreshejwe urupapuro rwabigenewe.[242]

Ikindi ni uko iyo umuntu yifuza ko umukozi wa Gasutamo akorera akazi ke mu kigo cye cyangwa ahandi hantu gasutamo idasanzwe ikorera, uwo muntu agomba kubisabira uruhushya, akoresheje inyandiko yabugenewe, ishyikirizwa umukozi ubishinzwe kandi hubahirijwe amategeko ndetse akishyura n'amafaranga asabwa kuri iyo mirimo; urwo ruhushya rugatangwa n'umukozi ubishinzwe kandi mu bushishozi bwe.[243] Abakomiseri ba

---

239 Itegeko rigenga za Gasutamo, umutwe wa II, 6(2).
240 Itegeko rigenga za Gasutamo, umutwe wa II, 7.
241 Itegeko rigenga za Gasutamo, umutwe wa II, 8(1).
242 Itegeko rigenga za Gasutamo, umutwe wa II, 8(2).
243 Itegeko rigenga za Gasutamo, umutwe wa II, 8(3)

za gasutamo z'ibihugu bigize umuryango basabwa kandi guhanahana amakuru no kugenzurira hamwe ibikorwa byo ku mupaka, mu rwego rwo kurwanya no guhashya magendu ndetse n'imikorere myiza ya za gasutamo muri rusange.[244] Ubufatanye hagati y'ibihugu bigize umuryango ni ingirakamaro cyane, kuko kurwanya magendu bisaba ubufatanye hagati y'ibihugu.

I.2. Ibijyanye n'inshingano zo kwishyura amahoro ya gasutamo

Nk'uko biteganywa n'Inyandikofatizo (*protocol*) yerekeye ishyirwaho ry'Ubumwe bwa za Gasutamo z'Umuryango wa Afurika y'Iburasirazuba, ijambo "amahoro" risobanura umusoro wose ucibwa hashingiwe ku mategeko ya gasutamo.[245] Ibi bigaragaza neza ko amahoro acibwa gusa ku bintu byinjira cyangwa bisohoka mu gihugu; bityo akaba adakwiye kwitiranywa n'imisoro y'imbere mu gihugu nk'umusoro ku nyongeragaciro, umusoro ku nyungu, n'indi misoro misoro icibwa hashingiwe ku mategeko atari aya gasutamo. Amategeko agenga za gasutamo agena ibipimo n'ikigero cy'amahoro yishyurwa ku bicuruzwa byinjira mu gihugu kigize umuryango biturutse mu kindi gihugu kigize umuryango cyangwa hanze yawo. Ayo mategeko kandi ateganya ibijyanye n'inshingano zo kwishyura amahoro, ndetse n'ubusonerwe bw'amahoro ku bicuruzwa bimwe na bimwe.

---

[244] Itegeko rigenga za Gasutamo, umutwe wa II, 10.

[245] Ingingo ya 1 y'Inyandikofatizo (*protocol*) yerekeye ishyirwaho ry'Ubumwe bwa za Gasutamo z'Umuryango wa Afurika y'Iburasirazuba, 2004. Reba kandi A.S. Hornby, "*Oxford learner's dictionary of current English*", 8th ed., Oxford University Press, p. 457.

I.2.1. Ibipimo by'amahoro

Amahoro atangwa ku bicuruzwa, hakurikijwe urutonde n'impamvu ziteganijwe mu Nyandikofatizo (*Protocol*) yerekeye ishyirwaho rya za gasutamo z'umuryango wa Afurika y'Iburasirazuba.[246] Iyo, hubahirijwe ingingo zikubiye mu itegeko ribigenga, ibicuruzwa bitangwaho amahoro, bisohotse mu gihugu kigize umuryango, byaba byarakorewe koherezwa mu mahanga cyangwa gukoreshwa ikindi kintu, ibyo bicuruzwa bigomba kugengwa n'itegeko rigenga za gasutamo, nk'aho bisohotse mu gihugu kigize umuryango, byaboneyemo uruhushya rubyohereza mu mahanga.[247]

I.2.2. Uko ibipimo by'amahoro byubahirizwa mu muryango

Ibicuruzwa bifite inkomoko mu bihugu bigize umuryango bisoreshwa hakurikijwe ibipimo by'amahoro y'umwihariko y'umuryango, nkuko biteganywa mu mategeko agenga inkomoko y'ibicuruzwa akubiye mu Nyandikofatizo; gasutamo ikaba igomba gusaba kwerekwa icyemezo cy'inkomoko y'ibicuruzwa n'izindi nyandiko zisobanura neza aho ibicuruzwa bikomoka.[248]

Ibipimo by'amahoro y'umwihariko bikoreshwa ku bicuruzwa bitumizwa, mu rwego rw'amasezerano hagati ya COMESA[249] na SADC[250], n'ibihugu bigize umuryango

---

246 "Inyandikofatizo"(*Protocol*) ni amasezerano yerekeye ishyirwaho ry'Ubumwe bwa za Gasutamo z'Umuryango wa Afurika y'Iburasirazuba n'imigereka yayo (Itegeko rigenga za Gasutamo, Umutwe wa I, 2.)

247 Itegeko rigenga za Gasutamo, Umutwe wa X, 110.

248 Itegeko rigenga za Gasutamo, Umutwe wa X, 111.

249 "COMESA" bisobanuye Umuryango w'Isoko Rusange ry'Afurika y'Iburasirazuza n'iy'Amajyepfo washyizweho n'amasezerano yo muri 1994. Reba kandi UNCTAD, "*Competition policy, trade and development in the Common Market for Eastern and Southern Africa*

nkuko biteganijwe mu mategeko ya buri gihugu kigize umuryango; bitumizwa, mu rwego rw'amasezerano yerekeye ibipimo by'amahoro y'umwihariko, ashobora kuba yaremejwe n'Inama y'Abaminisitiri.[251]

I.3. Isonerwa ry'amahoro

Isonerwa ry'amahoro rivugwa muri iki gice riri mu byiciro bibiri. Ibicuruzwa bimwe, mu gihe byinjiye muri kimwe mu bihugu bigize umuryango, ntibyishyura amahoro; mu gihe ibindi byinjira mu gihugu bidatanzweho amahoro, ariko igihe cyo kubirekura bikagira ayo bitanga.

I.3.1. Ibicuruzwa bisonewe amahoro

Amahoro ntagomba kwakwa ku bicuruzwa biri ku rutonde ruri mu Mutwe A w'umugereka wa gatanu w'itegeko rigenga za gasutamo, iyo ibyo bicuruzwa byatumijwe cyangwa byaguzwe mbere y'uko bikorerwa imenyekanisha muri gasutamo, rituma bijya gukoreshwa n'umuntu uvugwa muri uwo mutwe, kandi hubahirijwe amabwiriza y'umwihariko akubiyemo.[252] Amahoro kandi ntagomba kwakwa ku bicuruzwa biri ku rutonde ruri mu Mutwe B w'umugereka wa gatanu w'itegeko rigenga za gasutamo, iyo ibyo bicuruzwa byatumijwe, hubahirijwe amabwiriza y'umwihariko akubiye muri uwo mutwe.[253]

(COMESA), United Nations, Geneva, 2000, at www.unctad.org, accessed on 4 November 2014.

250 "SADC" ni Umuryango utsura Amajyambere mu Bihugu bya Afurika y'Amajyepfo, *ibidem.*

251 Itegeko rigenga za Gasutamo, Umutwe wa X, 111.

252 Ibicuruzwa bivugwa mu mutwe A umugereka wa gatanu w'itegeko rigenga za gasutamo, ni Ibicuruzwa byatumijwe cyangwa byaguzwe mbere y'imenyekanisha rikorwa n'abantu ku giti cyabo cyangwa mu izina ryabo n'imiryango ifite ubudahangarwa.

253 Ibi bicuruzwa bivugwa mu mutwe B umugereka wa gatanu w'itegeko rigenga za gasutamo ni ibicuruzwa byatumijwe cyangwa byaguzwe mbere yo kwerekanwa muri Gasutamo, aribyo: kontineri n'ibikoresho byo guterekaho ibicuruzwa; imizigo/ibikoressho

Itegeko rigenga za gasutamo kandi riha inama y'abaminisitiri, ibicishije mu igazeti y'umuryango, ububasha bwo gufata icyemezo cyo gukora ubugororangingo ku mugereka wa gatanu wavuzwe haruguru.[254]

Itegeko rigenga za gasutamo kandi risonera amahoro ibi bintu bikurikira[255]:

a. Ibicuruzwa byakorewe imenyekanisha rituma byoherezwa mu mahanga;
b. Ibicuruzwa byagumye mu kintu kibitwaye; nk'indege cyangwa ubwato;
c. Ibicuruzwa byakorewe imenyekanisha rituma byoherezwa mu mahanga;
d. Ibicuruzwa bimwe na bimwe bigaruka mu gihugu (*re-imports*);
e. ibyinjira ku bicuruzwa byatumijwe mu mahanga by'agateganyo;
f. Ibicuruzwa byeguriwe Leta, bigomba gutangwaho amahoro;

---

y'umuntu witabye Imana; Amafi, ingaru n'ibiyamunjongo byarobwe kandi bitwawe n'amato yanditse muri kimwe mu bihugu bigize umuryango; imizigo n'ibikoresho by'abagenzi byujuje ibisabwa n'uyu mugereka; ibyitegererezo n'utundi ducogocogo (samples and miscellaneous articles); ubwato; imiti yo kwoza ibikoresho byo mu ikaragiro; inzitiramibu n'ibikoresho bivamo inzitiramibu; imbuto zo gutera/kubiba; uruvange rw'ibikoreshwa ubutabire bwerekanye ko byakoreshwa nk'ifumbire; inzu ndangamurage, ibihangano birimo n'ibikoresho; udufuka tujyamo inkari n'udufuka dusa natwo tw'isuku cyangwa dukoreshwa mu buvuzi hakurikijwe ingano igenwa na Komiseri; Imiti ikoreshwa mu gusuzuma uburwayi; amashitingi akoreshwa mu buhinzi busanzwe, mu busitani no mu buhinzi bw'indabyo;ibikorerwa indege; ibikoreshofatizo byo gukora imiti; ibikoresho by'uburezi biteganywa mu masezerano ya Florence;

254 Itegeko rigenga za Gasutamo, Umutwe wa X, 114 (3).

255 Itegeko rigenga za Gasutamo, Umutwe wa X, 113-118.

I.3.2. Ibicuruzwa byinjira mu gihugu bidatanzweho amahoro, ariko igihe cyo kubirekura bikagira ayo bitanga

Iyo ibicuruzwa bigomba gutangirwa amahoro ku byinjira, byatumijwe mu mahanga, cyangwa bikaba byaraguzwe mbere yo gukorerwa imenyekanisha rituma bijya gukoreshwa mu gihugu n'umuntu cyangwa mu izina ry'umuntu, ufite ubusonerwe cyangwa wemerewe gutanga amahoro ku gipimo kiri hasi, kandi ibyo bicuruzwa bikaba nyuma, bishobora gukoreshwa ku buryo bunyuranye n'impamvu yatumye bisonerwa amahoro ; ibyo bicuruzwa bigomba, igihe cyo kujya gukoreshwa, kwishyura amahoro, hakurikijwe igipimo gikoreshwa ku bindi bicuruzwa byo mu rwego rumwe cyangwa se ibihwanije nabyo inyito, igihe cyo kujya kubikoresha; keretse amahoro atagomba gutangwa, igihe cyo gutwara ibyo bicuruzwa (iyo nyirabyo aramutse ari umuntu usanzwe), witabye Imana kandi ibyo bicuruzwa bikaba bitakimwanditseho kubera ko byarazwe, cyangwa byazunguwe n'undi muntu.[256]

Iyo ibicuruzwa, birebwa n'ingingo zikubiye mu mu mutwe wa X, 119 (1) z'itegeko rya gasutamo byavuzwe mu gika kibanziriza iki, byemerewe kugenda, icyo gihe, umuntu wemerewe kubitwara, agomba gushyikiriza Komiseri ibimenyetso by'umwihariko, byerekeye uruhushya rwo kubitwara kandi akishyura amahoro yose yerekeye ibyo bicuruzwa.[257]

Umuntu wese kandi utwara cyangwa akagura ibicuruzwa birebwa n'ingingo zikubiye mu mutwe wa X, 119 (1) z'itegeko rya gasutamo atabitangiye amahoro abisabwaho,

---

[256] Itegeko rigenga za Gasutamo, Umutwe wa X, 119 (1)
[257] Itegeko rigenga za Gasutamo, Umutwe wa X, 119 (2)

nkuko biteganijwe mu ngingo zikubiye muri iki cyiciro, aba akoze icyaha.[258]

Iyo ibicuruzwa birebwa n'ingingo zikubiye mu ngingo yavuzwe mu gika kibanza, bitwawe bidatangiwe amahoro ku byinjira abisabwaho, ibyo bicuruzwa bihanishwa gufatirwa burundu.[259]

I.4. Kurwanya magendu

Imwe mu mpamvu z'ingenzi zituma habaho ubufanye mu bya gasutamo hagati y'ibihugu ni ukurwanya cyangwa kugabanya ubucuruzi bwa magendu muri rusange.[260] Nk'uko biteganywa n'Itegeko rigenga za gasutamo, magendu ni ugutumiza, kwohereza, kunyuza, kwimurira cyangwa gutwara imbere cyangwa hanze y'ibihugu bigize umuryango, ibicuruzwa ugambiriye kunyereza amahoro, cyangwa guhunga amabwiriza aca, akumira cyangwa abuza gutumiza, kwohereza hanze, kunyuza mu gihugu, kwimurira cyangwa gutwara ibicuruzwa nk'ibyo.[261]

Zimwe mu ngingo z'itegeko rigenga za gasutamo zigamije kurwanya magendu n'ubucuruzi budakurikije amategeko hagati y'ibihugu bigize umuryango w'ibihugu by'afurika y'iburasirazuba. Iryo tegeko riha ububasha bumwe na bumwe abakozi ba gasutamo, mu rwego rwo kubafasha kugenzura magendu.

Nk'uko byavuzwe haruguru, umukozi wa gasutamo uri mu kazi ke ahabwa ububasha n'uburenganzira nk'ubw'umugenzacyaha wa polisi. Mu rwego rwo kurwanya magendu, uyu mukozi afite ububasha bwo kwinjira mu bwato cyangwa indege no kubisaka, mu gihe

[258] Itegeko rigenga za Gasutamo, Umutwe wa X, 119 (3)

[259] Itegeko rigenga za Gasutamo, Umutwe wa X, 119 (4)

[260] V. Ogalo, "*Informal Cross Border Trade in East African Community/Implications for regional integration and development*", CUTS African Resource Centre, Research Paper, 2010, p. 2.

[261] Itegeko rigenga za Gasutamo, Umutwe wa I, 2.

biri muri kimwe mu bihugu bigize umuryango; kubimarana igihe runaka mu rwego rw'akazi, ndetse no kubitegeka kuva mu gihugu.[262] Ashobora kandi gufatira ibihano umuderevu w'indege cyangwa ubwato wakoze icyaha.[263]

Umukozi wa gasutamo kandi afite ububasha bwo gusaka amazu; gukora amarondo; kwinjira ahantu aho ariho hose no gusaka no kuhagenzura nta nkomyi, mu rwego rwo kurwanya magendu.[264] Uyu mukozi kandi afite ububasha bwo guhagarika imodoka icyekwaho gutwara ibicuruzwa bya magendu no kuyisaka; ndetse no gufatira ibikoresho bijyanye n'icyaha.[265]

Abagenzi bajya mu bihugu bigize umuryango bategetswe gusubiza ibibazo byerekeye imizigo yabo, no kwerekana impapuro bijyanye.[266] Umukozi wa gasutamo kandi afite ububasha bwo gusaka abantu bakekwaho magendu, no gufata umuntu iyo hari impamvu zifatika zigaragaza ko umuntu ari gukora cyangwa yafashije undi gukora icyaha.[267]

I.5. Ikemurampaka ku bibazo bijyanye n'amategeko agenga gasutamo

Ibibazo byose bijyanye no kutubahiriza amategeko ya gasutamo bikemurwa mu buryo bubiri (2). Bishobora gukemurwa na komiseri hakoreshejwe inzira y'ubwumvikane cyangwa bigakemurwa n'inkiko zibifitiye ububasha.[268]

262 Itegeko rigenga za Gasutamo, Umutwe wa XII, 149-150.
263 Itegeko rigenga za Gasutamo, Umutwe wa XII, 150.
264 Itegeko rigenga za Gasutamo, Umutwe wa XII, 150-151.
265 Itegeko rigenga za Gasutamo, Umutwe wa XII, 153.
266 Itegeko rigenga za Gasutamo, Umutwe wa XII, 154.
267 Itegeko rigenga za Gasutamo, Umutwe wa XII, 155-156.
268 E. Kafeero, *op.cit.*, p. 65.

I.5.1. Ikemurampaka rikozwe na Komiseri

Iyo bigaragara ko umuntu yakoze icyaha, giteganijwe n'itegeko rigenga za gasutamo, gihanishwa ihazabu yateganijwe, cyangwa iyo ikintu giteganyirijwe igihano cyo gufatirwa burundu, Komiseri ashobora gucyemura icyo kibazo mu bwumvikane, kandi agategeka uwo muntu kwishyura umubare w'amafaranga, utarenze uw'ihazabu yaciwe, asanga ikwiranye n'igihano yari guhabwa, iyo uwo muntu aza kuba yararezwe mu rukiko kandi akaba yarahawe igihano gihwanye n'icyo cyaha.[269] Komiseri ashobora kandi gutegeka ko ikintu cyatumye hakorwa icyaha, giteganirijwe igihano cyo gufatirwa burundu, cyigihabwa.[270]

Komiseri ariko ntiyemerewe gukoresha ububasha ahabwa n'ingingo zikubiye mu gika kibanza, keretse umuntu yemeye mu nyandiko yabugenewe, ko yakoze icyaha kandi amusaba ko yahanirwa icyo cyaha, nkuko biteganijwe mu ngingo zikubiye muri iki cyiciro.[271]

Iyo Komiseri agomba gufata icyemezo mu bwumvikane: (a) icyo cyemezo kigomba gushyirwa mu nyandiko kandi cyikwomekwa ku nyandiko isaba gusuzuma ikibazo, cyashyikirijwe Komiseri na nyir'ubwite ; (b) icyo cyemezo kigomba kugaragaza neza icyaha cyakozwe n'uwo muntu n'igihano yahawe na Komiseri ; (c) uwo muntu agomba guhabwa kopi y'icyo cyemezo, iyo ayisabye ; (d) ntagomba kwongera gukurikiranwa kubera icyo cyaha ; iyo bibaye, kiriya cyemezo kimubera ingingo nziza yo kwireguza, kuko aba afite gihamya y'uko icyaha aregwa, cyacyemuwe ku bwumvikane, hubahirijwe ingingo zateganijwe muri iki cyiciro; (e) icyo cyemezo

---

[269] Itegeko rigenga za Gasutamo, Umutwe wa XVIII, 219 (1)
[270] *Ibidem.*
[271] *Ibidem.*

kiba ari ntakuka kandi ntikijuririrwa ndetse gishobora no gushyirwa mu bikorwa.[272]

I.5.2. Kugeza ikirego mu rukiko

Hatabangamiwe ububasha bw'urukiko rubifitiye ubushobozi, ikirego cyerekeye icyaha, giteganijwe mu itegeko rigenga za gasutamo, gishobora kuburanishwa kandi kigacyemurirwa mu rukiko rw'ibanze; iyo ruburanishije kandi rugaca urubanza, urwo rukiko rugomba kuba rufite n'ubushobozi bwo gutanga igihano cy'ihazabu cyangwa igihano cyo gufungwa, giteganijwe n'iri tegeko, ku muntu icyaha cyahamye.[273] Uretse kandi iyo byateganijwe ukundi ku bwende, umuntu wese warezwe mu rukiko, kubera icyaha giteganijwe n'itegeko ryavuzwe haruguru, agomba kuburanishwa, hakurikijwe ingingo zikubiye mu gitabo cy'amategeko agenga imiburanishirize y'imanza mpanabyaha, akoreshwa mu gihugu kigize umuryango, urwo rukiko rurimo.[274]

I.6. Ubujurire

Ubujurire buvugwa aha bukorwa mu nzego ebyiri (2): kujuririra Komiseri no kujuririra inkiko mu gihe uwajuririye Komiseri atanyuzwe n'icyemezo cyafashwe.

1.5.1. Kujuririra Komiseri

Umuntu utanyuzwe n'icyemezo kimureba cya Komiseri cyangwa undi mukozi wa gasutamo; cyangwa ntibite ku kibazo cye, ku byerekeye ibibazo bya gasutamo, afite uburenganzira bwo kujuririra icyo cyemezo cyangwa uko kutitabwaho, mu gihe kitarenze iminsi mirongo itatu (30), uhereye ku itariki icyo cyemezo cyafatiwe cyangwa cyititaweho. Ubwo bujurire bugomba gushyikirizwa Komiseri mu nyandiko kandi bugasobanura neza impamvu bwashingiyeho[275]

---

[272] Itegeko rigenga za Gasutamo, Umutwe wa XVIII, 219 (3)
[273] Itegeko rigenga za Gasutamo, Umutwe wa XVIII, 220 (1)
[274] Itegeko rigenga za Gasutamo, Umutwe wa XVIII, 220 (3)
[275] Itegeko rigenga za Gasutamo, Umutwe wa XVIII, 229 (1)

Iyo Komiseri anyuzwe n'ibisobanuro bikurikira: kuba atari mu gihugu kigize umuryango, uburwayi bwe cyangwa indi mpamvu, yatumye umuntu utaranyuzwe n'icyemezo cya Komiseri cyangwa kutamwitaho atamushyikiriza ubujurire mu gihe giteganywa n'itegeko, kandi bikaba byaragaragaye ko uko gukererwa kutaturutse ku burangare bwe, komiseri ashobora kwakira ubwo bujurire, yashyikirijwe nyuma y'igihe ntarengwa giteganywa n'itegeko.[276]

Komiseri agomba kumenyesha uwajuriye, icyemezo cye mu nyandiko, asobanura n'impamvu zatumye agifata, mu gihe kitarenze iminsi mirongo itatu (30), uhereye ku itariki yashyikirijweho ubujurire, n'andi makuru y'inyongera ashobora gusaba uwajuriye.[277]

Iyo atashoboye kumenyesha uwajuriye icyemezo yafashe mu gihe giteganijwe n'itegeko, komiseri afatwa nk'aho yemeye ubwo bujurire.[278] Mu gihe kandi hagitegerejwe igisubizo ku bujurire yashyikirijwe, komiseri ashobora, abisabwe n'uwajuriye, kurekura ibicuruzwa byose byajuriririwe, nyuma y'uko hishyuwe amahoro asabwa na komiseri cyangwa hatanzwe ingwate ihagije yo kwishingira amahoro n'ihazabu izatangwa, nkuko bigaragazwa n'imibare ya komiseri.[279]

---

276 Itegeko rigenga za Gasutamo, Umutwe wa XVIII, 229 (3)
277 Itegeko rigenga za Gasutamo, Umutwe wa XVIII, 229 (4)
278 Itegeko rigenga za Gasutamo, Umutwe wa XVIII, 229 (5)
279 Itegeko rigenga za Gasutamo, Umutwe wa XVIII, 229 (6)

I.5.2. Kujuririra urukiko

Umuntu utanyuzwe n'icyemezo yafatiwe na Komiseri, ashobora kujuririra icyo cyemezo mu rukiko rw'imisoro rwashyizweho hashingiwe ku itegeko rigenga za gasutamo.[280] Umuntu ufite igitekerezo cyo kujurira, agomba kubikora mu minsi mirongo ine n'itanu (45), nyuma yo kumenyeshwa icyo cyemezo, kandi akagenera komiseri kopi y'ubwo bujurire.[281]

Itegeko rigenga za gasutamo riteganya ko haseguriwe amategeko akoreshwa mu bihugu bigize Umuryango, ku byerekeye ubujurire bw'ibirebana n'imisoro, buri gihugu kigize umuryango, kigomba gushyiraho urukiko rwihariye rushinzwe gusuzuma ubujurire bwerekeye ibyemezo.[282]

N'ubwo itegeko riteganya ibyo, kugeza ubu nta rukiko rwihariye rushinzwe gusuzuma ubujurire bw'ibirebana n'imisoro ruri mu Rwanda; kuko imanza z'imisoro zose, ku nzego zose, ziburanishwa n'inkiko z'ubucuruzi,[283] hamwe n'urukiko rw'ikirenga.[284]

Ntitwasoza iki gice tutavuze ko mu rwego rwo gushyira mu bikorwa amategeko agenga za gasutamo[285], u Rwanda

---

[280] Itegeko rigenga za Gasutamo, Umutwe wa XVIII, 230 (1)

[281] Itegeko rigenga za Gasutamo, Umutwe wa XVIII, 230 (2)

[282] Itegeko rigenga za Gasutamo, Umutwe wa XVIII, 231

[283] Ingingo ya 3 y'Itegeko n° 59/2007 ryo ku wa 16/12/2007 rishyiraho inkiko z'ubucuruzi, rikanagena imitunganyirize, imikorere n'ububasha bwazo;

[284] *Urukiko rw'ikirenga rufite ububasha bwo kuburanisha ku rwego rw'ubujurire imanza zaciwe ku rwego rwa mbere n'Urukiko Rukuru rw'Ubucuruzi. (Ibi bishatse kuvuga ko n'imanza z'imisoro zaciwe n'Urukiko Rukuru rw'Ubucuruzi ku rwego rwa mbere, ziburanishwa n'Urukiko rw'Ikirenga ku rwego rw'ubujurire*). Reba ingingo ya 28 y'Itegeko n° 03/2012/OL ryo ku wa 13/06/2012 rigena imiterere, imikorere n'ububasha by'Urukiko rw'Ikirenga, *O.G.* yo ku wa 09/7/2012.

[285] Itegeko rigenga za Gasutamo, Umutwe wa I, 2.

rwagiye rusinya amasezerano y'ubwumvikane ku rwego rw'umuryango ajyanye no gushyiraho ibiro bihuriweho n'ibihugu ku mipaka (*one stop border post*) hagamijwe kworohereza abakora ubucuruzi, ndetse n'urujya n'uruza rw'ibintu n'abantu mu Rwanda no mu muryango muri rusange.[286] Abantu binjira cyangwa binjiza ibicuruzwa byabo mu Rwanda baturutse mu bihugu byasinyanye bene ayo masezerano n'u Rwanda bakaba boroherezwa mu kubona serivisi zose bakenera mu gihe cyo kwinjira mu gihugu, harimo na serivisi zijyanye n'imisoro. U Rwanda kandi rwashyizeho agace k'ubuhahirane gasonewe imisoro n'amahoro (*Free Trade Zone*), aho ibicuruzwa biva mu mahanga byinjira muri ako gace bidatanzweho imisoro n'amahoro; igice kinini cyabyo kikagurishwa kigamije kwongera kwoherezwa mu mahanga.[287] Ibi bikaba bigamije kuzamura urwego rw'ishoramali mu Rwanda no mu bihugu bigize umuryango muri rusange.

II. Amasezerano yo kudasoresha kabiri

Nk'uko twabikomojeho hejuru, ibihugu bigize umurwango w'uburasirazuba byasinyanye amasezerano yo kudasoresha kabiri ku musaruro winjijwe n'umuntu uri (*resident*) muri kimwe mu bihugu bigize umuryango. Amasezerano yo kudasoresha inshuro ebyiri ni ingirakamaro cyane ku bihugu byayasinyanye, kuko ku ruhande rumwe agira uruhare rukomeye mu iterambere ry' ishoramali hagati y'ibihugu byayasinye; ndetse ku rundi ruhande agafasha ubuyobozi bw'imisoro kugirana ubufatanye mu kurwanya inyerezwa ry'imisoro hagati

---

[286]East African Legislative Assembly, "*EAC One Stop Border Post Bill, 2012, inches a step closer to law*", available at www.eala.org, accessed at 5 November 2014.

[287]Reba ingingo ya 2 y'itegeko n° 26/2005 ryo kuwa 17/12/2005 rigamije guteza imbere no korohereza ishoramari n'ibicuruzwa byoherezwa mu mahanga, Igazeti

y'ibihugu byombi.[288] Urugero ni nko guhanahana amakuru hagati y'inzego zishinzwe kurwanya magendu mu bihugu bigize umuryango. Muri rusange kandi aya masezerano atanga ikizere ku bantu cyangwa amasosiyeti akorera muri kimwe mu bihugu bigize umuryango, kuko umusoro wishyuwe mu gihugu kimwe uhabwa agaciro mu kindi gihugu.

Aya masezerano yasinywe ku wa 30 Ugushyingo 2010, hagati y'ibihugu bigize umuryango aribyo u Rwanda, u Burundi, Kenya Uganda na Tanzania. Mu Rwanda, aya masezerano arebana gusa n'imisoro icibwa hashingiwe ku Itegeko n° 16/2005 ryo ku wa 18/08/2005 rigenga imisoro itaziguye ku musaruro[289], n'imisoro ku bukode bw'imitungo itimukanwa iteganywa n'Itegeko n° 17/2005 rigena inkomoko y'umutungo w'uturere n'imijyi n'icungwa ryawo.

Muri Kenya aya masezerano areba umusaruro usoreshwa hashingiwe ku Itegeko rigenga umusoro ku musaruro, Cap. 470[290]; muri Tanzaniya arebana n'imisoro icibwa hashingiwe ku Itegeko rigenga umusoro ku musaruro, Cap. 332[291], naho muri Uganda akarebana n'imisoro icibwa hashingiwe ku Itegeko rigenga umusoro ku

---

[288] A. Trepelkov, H. Tonino and D. Halka, *United Nations Handbook on Selected Issues in Administration of Double Tax Treaties for Developing Countries*, New York, 2013, p., iii. Reba kandi: United Nations, Department of Economic and Social Affairs, *United Nations Model Double Taxation Convention between Developed and Developing Countries,* New York: United Nations, 2011; Organisation for Economic Co-operation and Development, *Model Tax Convention on Income and on Capital*, Paris, OECD, 2010.

[289] Itegeko n° 16/2005 ryo ku wa 18/08/2005 rigenga imisoro itaziguye ku musaruro, kuri www.rra.gov.rw.

[290] Kenyan Income Tax Act Cap 470, 1973, kuri www.opac.library.strathmore.edu, accessed on 11/11/2014

[291] Tanzania Income Tax Act Cap 332, 2006, kuri www.tra.go.tz., accessed on 5/11/2014.

musaruro, Cap. 340[292]; mu gihe mu Burundi aya masezerano arebana n'imisoro icibwa hashingiwe ku itegeko rigenga umusoro ku nyungu ryo mu mwaka wa 1963.[293]

N'ubwo bimeze bityo, ishyirwa mu bikorwa ry'aya masezerano ntabwo ryashyizwemo ingufu na bimwe mu bihugu bigize umuryango, kuko kugeza ubu u Rwanda arirwo rwonyine rumaze gushyira umukono ku masezerano yemeza burundu ayo masezerano, kugira ngo atangire gukurikizwa[294] Bigaragara kandi ko ibihugu bigize umuryango bishyira ingufu nyinshi mu ishyirwamubikorwa ry'amasezerano yo kudasoresha kabiri bifitanye n'ibindi bihugu, kurenza uko byashyira mu bikorwa amasezerano byasinyanye hagati yabyo.

---

[292] Ugandan Income Tax Act Cap 340, 1997, kuri www.eac.int/customs.com, accessed on 5/11/2014.

[293] Loi relative aux impots sur les revenues de 1963, kuri www.afficade.com, accedé au 5/11/2014.

[294] Reba ingingo ya 190 y'Itegekonshinga rya Repubulika y'u Rwanda ryo ku wa 04 Kamena 2003 nk'uko ryavuguruwe kugeza ubu; PWC, "*Doing business: know your taxes*", East Africa Tax Guide 2011/2012, October 2011, p.2.

References

I. Legal Texts

0. Constitution of the Republic of Rwanda 04th June 2003 as amended to date, in *O.G.* n° special of 04th June 2003.
1. Agreement between the Republics of Rwanda, Burundi, Kenya, Uganda and the United Republic of Tanzania for the avoidance of double taxation and the prevention of fiscal evasion with respect to taxes on income of 30th November 2010
2. Organic Law n° 34/2007 of 13/08/2007 modifying and complementing the Organic Law n° 14/2004 of 26/05/2004 establishing general provisions governing public institutions, in *O.G.* n° 16 of 15/08/2004.
3. Organic law n° 37/2006 of 12/09/2006 on State finances and property, in *O.G.* n° special of 12/09/2006 as modified and complemented by Organic Law n° 65/2008 of 11/09/2008 in *O.G.* n° 24 of 15/12/2008.
4. Law n° 01/2012 of 03/02/2012 modifying and complementing law n° 25/2005 of 04/12/2005 on tax procedures as modified and complemented to date, in O.G. n° 13 of 26/03/2012.
5. Law n° 28/2012 of 27/07/2012 modifying and complementing the law n° 16/2005 on direct taxes on income as modified and complemented to date.
6. Law n° 25/2010 of 28/05/2010 modifying and complementing law n°06/2001 of 20/01/2001 on the Code of Value Added Tax.
7. Law n° 19/2009 of 30/06/2009 modifying and completing the law n° 26/2006 of 27/05/2006 determining and establishing consumption tax on some imported and locally manufactured products.

8. Law n° 74/2008 of 31/12/2008 modifying and complementing law n° 25/2005 of 04/12/2005 on tax procedures.
9. Law n° 73/2008 of 31/12/2008 modifying and complementing law n° 16/2005 of 18/08/2005 on direct taxes on income.
10. Law n° 16/2005 of 18/08/2005 on direct taxes on income.
11. Law n° 25/2005 of 04/12/2005 on tax procedures.
12. Law n° 33/2003 of 06/9/2003 modifying and complementing law n°17/2002 of 10/05/2002 establishing the source of revenue for districts and towns and its management.
13. Law n° 23/2002 of 10/07/2002 modifying and completing the law n°06 0f 20/01/2001 on the code of Value Added Tax.
14. Law n° 17/2002 of 10/05/2002 establishing the source of revenue for districts and towns and its management, modified and complemented by the law n° 33/2003 of 06/09/2003.
15. Law n° 06/2001 of 20/01/2001 on the Code of Value Added Tax.
16. Law n° 05/2011 of 21/03/2011 regulating special economic zones in Rwanda, in *O. G.* n° special of 30 march 2011.
17. Ministerial Order n° 008/2009 of 01/12/2009 determining the amount of registration fees for imported and already registered vehicles in Rwanda.
18. Commissioner General Rules n° 008/2009 of 07/12/2009 modifying and completing the Commissioner General Rules n° 002/2007 of 15/06/2007 implementing the law n° 25/2005 of 04/12/2005 on tax procedures.

II. Books & Journal articles

1. Clark, W. S., "Tax Incentives for Foreign Direct Investment: Empirical Evidence on Effects and Alternative Policy Options", *Canadian Tax Journal*, vol. 48, nº 4, 2000.
2. Dotun, P., "Corporate Tax Incentives and Economic Growth in Nigeria", *Tax News*, 1996, vol. 2, nº 1.
3. Evans, D. S., Garcia-Swart, D. D. & Martin-Keating, B. G., "The Failure of E-Commerce Businesses: A Surprise or Not?", *European Business Organization Law Review*, 2002.
4. HORNBY, A.S, "*Oxford learner's dictionary of current English*", 8th ed., Oxford University Press, 2010.
5. Klemm, A., *Causes, Benefits, and Risks of Business Tax Incentives*, IMF Working Paper, WP/09/21, 2009.
6. Olabisi, J., "Tax Incentive as a Catalyst for Economic Development in Nigeria", *JORIND*, December 2009, vol. 2, nº 2.
7. Piciotto, S., *International Business Taxation*, London, Claphan High Street, 1992.
8. Sacha Wunsch, V., "The Internet, Cross-border Trade in Services, and the GATS: Lessons from US-Gambling", *World Trade Review*, 2006.

III. Other documents

1. East African Community, "*EAC Customs Valuation Manual: A guide to the Customs of Valuation of Imported Goods in the East African Community*", Arusha, 2012.
2. East African Legislative Assembly, " *EAC One Stop Border Post Bill, 2012, inches a step closer to law*", available at www.eala.org, accessed at 5 November 2014;

3. IPAR, East African Taxation Project: Rwanda Country Case Study, June 2011.
4. KHORANA, S., KIMBUGWE, K. & PERDIKIS, N., "The *impact of tarrif reductions under the East African Community Customs Union: Intra-trade effects on Uganda*", Research Peper, Ecomod, 2007.
5. NCUBE, M., BRIXIOVA, Z. & MENG, Q.,"*Can intra-regional trade act as a global shock absorber in Africa?*", African Development Bank Group Working Paper Series, n°198, 2014.
6. Ngagi, A. M., *Cours de droit civil des obligations*, Manuel pour étudiants, Butare, Les éditions de l'Université Nationale du Rwanda, 2004.
7. Nikozitambirwa, "De l'Impot Ikoro", available at http://users.skynet.be/wihogora/niko-rmm-ikoro-020503.htm, accessed on 15th June 2011.
8. OECD Report: Harmful Tax Competition, An Emerging Global Issue, 1998.
9. OGALO, V., "*Informal Cross Border Trade in East African Community/Implications for regional integration and development*", CUTS African Resource Centre, Research Paper, 2010.
10. Organisation for Economic Co-operation and Development, "*Model Tax Convention on Income and on Capital*", Paris, OECD, 2010.
11. PWC, "*Doing business: know your taxes*", East Africa Tax Guide 2011/2012, October 2011.
12. *Rapport de l'Etude sur les Comptes Bancaires du Secteur Public*, GN & Partners, for MINECOFIN, October 2002.
13. Rwanda Revenue Authority, *Annual Activity Report for 2009/2010*, Kigali, September 2010.
14. TREPELKOV, A., TONINO, H. and HALKA, D., *United Nations Handbook on Selected Issues in*

Administration of Double Tax Treaties for Developing Countries, New York, 2013.

15. UNCTAD, "*Competition policy, trade and development in the Common Market for Eastern and Southern Africa (COMESA),* United Nations, Geneva, 2000, at www.unctad.org, accessed on 4 November 2014.
16. United Nations, "*United Nations Model Double Taxation Convention between Developed and Developing Countries",* New York: United Nations, 2011.

Rwanda

aux éditions L'Harmattan

Dernières parutions

STATISTIQUE(S) ET GÉNOCIDE AU RWANDA
La genèse d'un système de catégorisation «génocidaire»
Tesfaye Facil
L'auteur propose ici une approche originale et novatrice, qu'il appellera «démo-statistique», du génocide rwandais de 1994. Cela lui permet de clarifier les liens qui existent entre les statistiques coloniales et le génocide et, ainsi, de «discuter l'indiscutable». Il s'intéresse notamment aux recensements démographiques lors du processus de création d'identité ainsi que pendant des conflits d'ordre ethnique.
(Coll. Justice Internationale, 15.50 euros, 154 p.)
ISBN : 978-2-343-04676-1, ISBN EBOOK : 978-2-336-36052-2

OPÉRATION (L') DE PAIX DES NATIONS UNIES AU RWANDA
Bidoung Noël
Dans la soirée du 6 avril 1994, un missile sol-air frappe de plein fouet l'avion présidentiel rwandais : tous les occupants, dont les chefs d'État rwandais et burundais, périssent dans l'attentat. La confusion et le chaos qui suivent sont le point de départ du génocide des Tutsis et de l'assassinat d'innombrables Hutus modérés. Mais où donc était la communauté internationale ? Et jusqu'à quand a-t-on laissé des centaines de milliers de personnes se faire massacrer en toute impunité ?
(13.50 euros, 120 p.)
ISBN : 978-2-336-29942-6, ISBN EBOOK : 978-2-336-35709-6

RWANDA 1994-2014
L'Église et la société dans la tourmente face au génocide
(essai de sociothérapie)
Nshogoza François-Xavier
En 1994, le Rwanda a connu une crise sociale qui s'est soldée par le génocide des Tutsi. Huit cent mille personnes furent victimes de cette tragédie, en cent jours. Dans la recherche des causes, certains considèrent que l'Église du Rwanda a contribué à maintenir divisée la nation. Nous voulons aller au-delà du sens commun pour arriver à la réalité du phénomène social. Le génocide n'étant pas une crise ecclésiale mais sociale, la sociothérapie à proposer regarde la société rwandaise entière.
(Harmattan Italia, 33.35 euros, 300 p.)
ISBN : 978-2-336-30700-8, ISBN EBOOK : 978-2-336-35497-2

SETH SENDASHONGA 1951-1998
Un Rwandais pris entre deux feux
Sous la direction d'André Guichaoua
Préface de Stephen Smith
Ce livre honore la mémoire d'un Rwandais, Seth Sendashonga, qui s'est battu contre deux dictatures : celle qui a précédé et celle qui a suivi le génocide de 1994. Sa publication coïncide avec le quinzième anniversaire de son meurtre (le 16 mai 1998), mais prend date pour l'espoir que Sendashonga incarnait : celui d'un Rwanda où la vérité ne s'abîme plus dans le clivage hutu/tutsi.
(18.00 euros, 188 p.)
ISBN : 978-2-343-00861-5, ISBN EBOOK : 978-2-296-53663-0

RWANDA : UNE ÈRE NOUVELLE
Comprendre le travail de reconnaissance
Poreau Brice
En 2012, le Rwanda a connu de nombreux changements. Les mois de juin et juillet ont été riches en événements et en commémorations du génocide, comme la fin officielle des tribunaux locaux, les Gacaca. La réconciliation du pays a été proclamée. Est-ce pour autant réel sur le terrain ? Qu'en pensent les nouvelles générations ? Photographie instantanée de l'état du Rwanda en 2012, cet ouvrage pose la question du passé, mais aussi de l'avenir de ce pays magnifique de l'Afrique centrale.
(Coll. Etudes africaines, 12.00 euros, 104 p.)
ISBN : 978-2-296-99758-5, ISBN EBOOK : 978-2-296-51398-3

ONU (L') FACE AU GÉNOCIDE RWANDAIS
Le silence des machettes
Plauchut Agathe
Préface de Patrice Pourtal
En 1994, au coeur du génocide des Tutsi au Rwanda, l'opération de maintien de la paix illustra l'impuissance de la communauté internationale à faire face au crime du génocide. En adoptant une optique militaire et géostratégique pour appréhender le génocide rwandais, ce livre analyse de l'intérieur les limites et enjeux d'une mission de maintien de la paix dans une situation dramatique.
(Coll. Mondes en mouvement, 23.50 euros, 238 p.)
ISBN : 978-2-336-00577-5, ISBN EBOOK : 978-2-296-51136-1

CRISE RWANDAISE : ENJEUX ET PERSPECTIVES
Mendy Marcel
La crise rwandaise a projeté sous les phares de l'actualité africaine et mondiale une tragédie douloureuse. L'auteur s'intéresse aux événements survenus, mais en dissèque la trame événementielle pour mettre en scène le poids de l'histoire, la personnalité des acteurs, la question des réfugiés, la quête de la démocratie, les tentatives d'entente, l'étincelle qui mit le feu aux poudres, ses conséquences et la réaction de la communauté internationale.
(12.00 euros, 108 p.)
ISBN : 978-2-296-99519-2, ISBN EBOOK : 978-2-296-50322-9

MANUEL D'HISTOIRE POLITIQUE ET SOCIALE DU RWANDA CONTEMPORAIN (TOME 1)
Suivant le modèle Mgr Alexis Kagame
La révolution rwandaise et la Première République rwandaise
Mureme K. Bonaventure
Ce manuel relate et analyse les mobiles, les causes, les facteurs, les variables qualitatives explicatives, les effets induits directs et indirects et les conséquences de l'abolition de la noblesse séculaire tutsie en 1959 et du retour en force en 1994 de la noblesse tutsie moderne Abâkagâra. Ce volume traite de la révolution rwandaise, la Première République rwandaise et, *de facto*, l'évolution fatale du rapport des forces à la défaveur du premier et unique président de la Première République, Grégoire Kayibanda.
(Coll. Etudes africaines, 41.00 euros, 432 p.)
ISBN : 978-2-296-99314-3

MANUEL D'HISTOIRE POLITIQUE ET SOCIALE DU RWANDA CONTEMPORAIN (TOME 2)
Suivant le modèle Mgr Alexis Kagame
Du coup d'État militaire du 5 juillet 1973 au génocide
Mureme K. Bonaventure
Ce manuel étudie la partie contemporaine, à partir du 25 avril 1949, de la spirale de la violence rwandaise qui date du Ve siècle. Ce tome 2 analyse rigoureusement la tyrannie militaire sanguinaire de l'Akazu menée par Juvénal Habyalimana Rutemayeze, puis celle du Front patriotique rwandais (FPR).
(Coll. Etudes africaines, 45.00 euros, 872 p.)
ISBN : 978-2-296-99315-0

GÉNOCIDE (LE) RWANDAIS VU PAR *L'EXPRESS* ET *JEUNE AFRIQUE*
Mpereng Jerry
Préface de Georges Ngal
Ce travail consiste à revisiter le génocide rwandais à travers différents systèmes, modèles et «logiques d'interprétation» des journaux. C'est-à-dire une analyse comparative entre deux hebdomadaires, *L'Express* et *Jeune Afrique*, avec pour objectif de rechercher des catégories, des jugements, des discours, des commentaires rendant compte justement d'une manière spécifique d'interpréter l'événement.
(Coll. Pensée Africaine, 12.00 euros, 104 p.)
ISBN : 978-2-296-96719-9

L'HARMATTAN ITALIA
Via Degli Artisti 15; 10124 Torino

L'HARMATTAN HONGRIE
Könyvesbolt ; Kossuth L. u. 14-16
1053 Budapest

L'HARMATTAN KINSHASA
185, avenue Nyangwe
Commune de Lingwala
Kinshasa, R.D. Congo
(00243) 998697603 ou (00243) 999229662

L'HARMATTAN CONGO
67, av. E. P. Lumumba
Bât. – Congo Pharmacie (Bib. Nat.)
BP2874 Brazzaville
harmattan.congo@yahoo.fr

L'HARMATTAN GUINÉE
Almamya Rue KA 028, en face
du restaurant Le Cèdre
OKB agency BP 3470 Conakry
(00224) 657 20 85 08 / 664 28 91 96
harmattanguinee@yahoo.fr

L'HARMATTAN MALI
Rue 73, Porte 536, Niamakoro,
Cité Unicef, Bamako
Tél. 00 (223) 20205724 / +(223) 76378082
poudiougopaul@yahoo.fr
pp.harmattan@gmail.com

L'HARMATTAN CAMEROUN
BP 11486
Face à la SNI, immeuble Don Bosco
Yaoundé
(00237) 99 76 61 66
harmattancam@yahoo.fr

L'HARMATTAN CÔTE D'IVOIRE
Résidence Karl / cité des arts
Abidjan-Cocody 03 BP 1588 Abidjan 03
(00225) 05 77 87 31
etien_nda@yahoo.fr

L'HARMATTAN BURKINA
Penou Achille Some
Ouagadougou
(+226) 70 26 88 27

L'HARMATTAN SÉNÉGAL
10 VDN en face Mermoz, après le pont de Fann
BP 45034 Dakar Fann
33 825 98 58 / 33 860 9858
senharmattan@gmail.com / senlibraire@gmail.com
www.harmattansenegal.com

L'HARMATTAN BÉNIN
ISOR-BENIN
01 BP 359 COTONOU-RP
Quartier Gbèdjromèdé,
Rue Agbélenco, Lot 1247 I
Tél : 00 229 21 32 53 79
christian_dablaka123@yahoo.fr

Achevé d'imprimer par Corlet Numérique - 14110 Condé-sur-Noireau
N° d'Imprimeur : 119797 - Dépôt légal : juin 2015 - *Imprimé en France*

www.ingramcontent.com/pod-product-compliance
Lightning Source LLC
LaVergne TN
LVHW021237061026
849535LV00008B/3092
* 9 7 8 2 3 4 3 0 6 8 4 3 5 *